The B&R at Seventy-Five

The B&R at Seventy-Five

The B&R at Seventy-Five

A History of the
Badminton and Racquet Club
1924–1999

THE DUNDURN GROUP
TORONTO · OXFORD

Copyright © Mary Byers 2001

All rights reserved. No part of this publication may be reproduced, stored in a retrieval system, or transmitted in any form or by any means, electronic, mechanical, photocopying, recording, or otherwise (except for brief passages for purposes of review) without the prior permission of Dundurn Press. Permission to photocopy should be requested from the Canadian Copyright Licensing Agency.

Design: Jennifer Scott
Printer: Gandalf (Bryant)

Canadian Cataloguing in Publication Data

Byers, Mary, 1933–
  The Badminton and Racquet Club of Toronto

Includes bibliographical references and index.
ISBN 1-55002-353-5

1. Badminton and Racquet Club of Toronto – History. I. Title.

GV1007.6.C3B93 2001   796.345'06'0713541   C00-932808-4

1   2   3   4   5   04   03   02   01   00

We acknowledge the support of the *Canada Council for the Arts* and the *Ontario Arts Council* for our publishing program. We also acknowledge the financial support of the *Government of Canada* through the *Book Publishing Industry Development Program*, *The Association for the Export of Canadian Books*, and the *Government of Ontario* through the *Ontario Book Publishers Tax Credit* program.

Care has been taken to trace the ownership of copyright material used in this book. The author and the publisher welcome any information enabling them to rectify any references or credit in subsequent editions.

J. Kirk Howard, President

Printed and bound in Canada.
Printed on recycled paper.
www.dundurn.com

Photo Credits

All photos not credited are from the B&R Archives or on loan from members. Colour photos are by John de Visser.

University Avenue Armouries. City of Toronto Archives SC244, Item 1001.: 17

Toronto and York Radial Railway car. City of Toronto Archives/TTC Fonds. Trans Series, Item 721.: 18

Deer Park Section. Laying tracks. City of Toronto Archives/TTC Fonds Series 71, Item 61011.: 18

The Nunns family. The Toronto Star, August 16, 1989. Tony Bock.: 81

Staff photos: Eleanor O'Gorman: 108, Paul Dunning: 107 (right); Milan Jablonsky: 120 (left); Dana Rodziunas: 120 (right); John, Maria, Manfred and Lopes: 136 (top); David Brightling: 123; Staff Christmas Party: 143; Gorden Chiu and Quang Hoang: 145 by Walter Psotka Photography.

Dundurn Press
8 Market Street
Suite 200
Toronto, Ontario, Canada
M5E 1M6

Dundurn Press
73 Lime Walk
Headington, Oxford,
England
OX3 7AD

Dundurn Press
2250 Military Road
Tonawanda NY
U.S.A. 14150

The B&R at SeventyFive

Table of Contents

Introduction — Toronto and the St. Clair and Yonge Area in 1924 ... 9
Chapter One — The Man and the Game ... 13
Chapter Two — With a Few Friends ... 16
Chapter Three — An Explosion of Membership and Courts Full of Champions ... 24
Chapter Four — The Thirties ... 36
Chapter Five — The War Years ... 45
Chapter Six — Post-War — Time to Re-evaluate ... 50
Chapter Seven — The Golden Days of Squash ... 64
Chapter Eight — Derek Bocquet — Tennis, Squash, and his Juniors ... 76
Chapter Nine — Fifty Years and on to the Diamond Anniversary ... 89
Chapter Ten — The Car Barns Have Another Upgrade ... 102
Chapter Eleven — A Family Club for the Nineties ... 115
Remembering the Time — The 75th Anniversary ... 138
The Club Today — The Games Our Members Play ... 144
Appendix — Our Best Shots ... 148
Acknowledgements ... 199
Bibliography ... 201
Index ... 202

Toronto and the St. Clair and Yonge Area in 1924

Toronto in 1924 was a staid, orderly, and relatively quiet city sometimes known as the "City of Churches." Its muddy laneways were being paved and the common sight was now the automobile, which, along with the horse-drawn carriage, cluttered the narrow streets — a means of transportation in competition with the new (1921) Toronto Transportation Commission (four rides for twenty-five cents until 1951). To assist motorists and streetcars there was now an automatic traffic light, the first in the city, at the Bloor and Yonge intersection. Nightlife was almost non-existent and whatever excitement the twenties generated in Toronto was very much under control. The population was just over half a million and growing slowly.

The skyline was emerging from architects' drawings and would soon spring to life. Queen Victoria's British Empire set the standard by which every piece of work was judged, and so Toronto would soon boast the Bank of Commerce Tower, called the tallest building in the British Empire (completed in 1931), the Royal York Hotel, known as the Empire's largest hotel (opened in 1929), and the Union Station, opened by the Prince of Wales in 1927. The Royal Winter Fair had been showing horses and livestock in the Coliseum for two years and

Yonge Street looking south to St. Clair in 1922. Tracks for the Radial Railway which ran down the west side are being replaced by a double track in the centre for the newly formed TTC. The Dominion Bank (now Toronto Dominion) is on the north east corner. Behind the "Drugs" sign would be the Bank of Commerce on the south-west corner (now CIBC), both in the same location today.

would soon be absorbed into the Canadian National Exhibition grounds where merchants' wares were there for the sampling behind the imposing Princes' Gates. Nearby Sunnyside Amusement Park was attracting crowds to the city's boardwalk.

At the University of Toronto, Trinity College, the alma mater of many B&R members, would open its doors at a new location, on Hoskin Avenue, in 1925. The first dial telephone had just been introduced and sports fans would shortly be able to call to arrange a trip to the baseball stadium, completed in time for the local team's victory in the Little World Series of 1926. Canada's first radio station, CFCA, owned by the *Toronto Star*, had started operations in 1922 and the voice of Foster Hewitt was now heard broadcasting hockey games from the Mutual Street Arena. The Timothy Eaton Company and the Robert Simpson Company had both put out mail order catalogues that brought a world of glamour and practicality to those not able to visit the department stores in person. Nearby Bay Street was flexing its young muscles. Toronto had recently basked in a major medical advancement when Dr. Frederick Banting and Dr. Charles Best had isolated insulin as a treatment for diabetes.

Closer to the St. Clair and Yonge area the excitement in 1924 was of Sir Henry Pellatt's abandoning his "home," Casa Loma, after his wife's death the previous year. The furniture was auctioned in June, 1924, by Jenkins Art Gallery. Hunts' Restaurant served catered buffet lunch at the gallery all week. Perhaps some of the grander pieces made their way to the newly created village of Forest Hill. Havergal College had just purchased twenty-seven acres of farmland at Avenue Road and Lawrence Avenue and so Havergal-On-The-Hill, the junior school that had stood on the south side of St. Clair, west of Yonge, for thirteen years, would now make way for the new and stately Granite Club.

The St. Clair and Yonge intersection was in the area called Deer Park, the name from the forty-acre estate of the Heath family, located there in 1850 at the northwest corner of Yonge Street and the Third Concession Road [St. Clair]. Deer Park was divided in two by "The Hill," the upper part north of St. Clair and the lower section south of Summerhill. Deer wandered freely at the intersection in the mid-1800s and were fed by guests at the local hotel, John Dew's establishment at the northeast corner. Dew had operated a complex there of feed store, gristmill, and distillery since 1836. He served his whiskey and sold it to nearby hostelries at eight cents a quart. Michael O'Halloran ran Dew's inn and later acquired and moved it to the southwest corner, building it into the up-to-date twelve-room Deer Park Hotel. The hotel was, according to Joan Kinsella, in her *Walking Tour of Deer Park*, "surrounded by fields for football, quoits, and horse racing." Near all this sporting activity St. Michael's Cemetery was quietly established in 1855 to be joined shortly thereafter by St. Charles Separate School.

The area was home to some of Toronto's elite who chose "The Hill" and built grand homes there — Oaklands, home of wealthy retail merchant, John Macdonald, now De La Salle "Oaklands" College, and three homes that gave their names to the community as streets — William McMaster's "Rathnelly," "Woodlawn," built by William Blake, and "Summer Hill," on a 200 acre estate, built by stagecoach owner Charles Thompson, later the property of Larratt Smith. With improved streetcar transportation (the Metro line was electrified in 1890) neighbourhoods were established and access to the area was simplified. The Rosedale Hotel (later the Ports of Call) was a popular stopping spot. There were schools; Deer Park Public School, as well as the older St. Charles, churches; Christ Church Deer Park in the gore by Yonge Street, (this small part of Deer Park, bounded by Heath, Duggan, and Oriole Road was known as the town of Drummondville), Deer Park Presbyterian on St. Clair just west of Yonge (in the 1925 split it became Deer Park United with the Presbyterian stalwarts opening Calvin Presbyterian). Yorkminster Baptist followed, as did Our Lady of Perpetual Help. Mount Pleasant Cemetery was created in 1876. And, on Heath Street West, the Deer Park Sanatorium "for the subjects of inebriety or narcomania." It was later called Dr. Meyers' Private Hospital for Nervous Diseases. Deer Park was annexed to the City of Toronto in 1908 and soon there was a firehall on Balmoral, a public library on Yonge Street and streetcar service on St. Clair. Joan Kinsella notes that "The new St. Clair bridge was opened over the Vale of Avoca in 1925" giving access to John Moore's new subdivision, Moore Park. Streetcars could now cross the bridge to Mount Pleasant and turn north to Eglinton.

The Badminton and Racquet Club site, where workmen with wrecking equipment were moving in to start demolition of the old car barns, was in the midst of a burgeoning shopping district. On the west side of Yonge Street south of St. Clair, the area most immediate to the club, from St. Michael's Cemetery north to the corner, there were by 1925, after some vacant land, Alice and Nora Millinery, White and Sons Dyers, Billinghurst Fruit, Alfred Sheridan Florist, Mary Stuart Confectionery and, on the corner, the Canadian Bank of Commerce. Within a year the vacant land had been taken up by a baker, a delicatessen, a men's furnishings shop, the North Yonge Café, a drug store, Hunts Confectionery, and by 1927, a Frigidaire show room, a shop selling victrolas, a grocery store, and, of great interest to B&R ladies, The Trocadero Bowling Alley.

From the corner of St. Clair and Yonge west along St. Clair beside the bank were: a cigar, shoeshine and jewellery store, a real estate and insurance office, a hairdresser, a contractor and Havergal College. A landmark across the road, A.W. Miles Funeral Chapel, opened in 1927. On the northeast corner of the intersection stood the Dominion Bank. Seventy-five years later, the same two banks (now the Canadian Imperial Bank of Commerce and the Toronto Dominion Bank) face each other across the street. By the end of the decade St. Clair and Yonge had achieved a certain amount of notoriety for a new arrival. The Hollywood Theatre had opened, one of the first motion picture theatres in Canada built specifically for the new rage, sound movies. To all this activity was now added the five hundred members of the Badminton and Racquet Club of Toronto.

The Man and the Game

"I don't think there is any doubt that without George Blackstock this club would never have been formed. We played at the old Toronto Armories from 1910 to 1924 [it closed during the war] and Blackstock was kicking my backside every week to get out and get something decent to play on — the floor was terrible — the conditions were not good…. We started a campaign to go around looking for some place that we might form a club…. We started practically on a shoestring. It took me nights and days to figure out what membership we could achieve from the old Toronto Garrison Badminton Club, The Toronto Racquet Club, of which I was a member, and The Winter Club, to get enough members and money to start this club."

Roy Buchanan

"Most of my contemporaries were playing squash at The University Club. Badminton was pioneered by the group at the armories. Blackstock got all his friends working."

Graeme Watson

"Canadians like strenuous sports. They have triumphed in both sprint and marathon running and they produce the best hockey players for many nations. So, when they discovered that badminton was not a la-de-da sort of game…. [T]hey took it to their bosoms and adopted it….The thud of shuttlecocks on tightly stretched gut began to echo across Canada, until today [1935] it resounds boldly from the walls of foreign clubs as Canadians sweep down any opposition to their conquering march. Canada is at the top of the badminton heap."

Jack Purcell, unofficial world professional badminton champion, who played many times on the B&R courts in the 1930s, and 40s, and into the 50s.

The rage in racquet sports was badminton. The driving force was Lieutenant-Colonel George Gooderham Blackstock, OBE, MC. In 1924 the combination led to the founding of the Badminton and Racquet Club of Toronto.

George Blackstock, one of eight children of Harriet Victoria Gooderham and Thomas Gibbs Blackstock, was a graduate of Upper Canada College and The Royal Military

College. He was a top athlete in football, hockey, and cricket. Quarterback for three years of the RMC football team and captain in his final year, he led the team to the Intermediate Dominion Finals against Hamilton (the Hamilton papers called him "some speed merchant") and to a major confrontation with the Varsity Seniors, all with such success that RMC entered the Senior Intercollegiate Football League in 1913. On graduation from RMC Blackstock went to the University of Toronto where he played on the 1913 Varsity team.

When war broke out George Blackstock joined the Royal Field Artillery, transferred to the Canadian Field Artillery, and saw action in England and France. He was appointed Lieutenant-Colonel in 1918 at age 26. That year he was awarded the Military Cross, and the following year the Order of the British Empire, in which citation he was commended for "fearlessness and disregard for self under shell fire." He was twice mentioned in Dispatches.

After the war, as executive vice-president of Steep Rock Mines, Blackstock played an important part in the development of the mining industry in Canada. In March, 1943 he visited the lakehead to look at mining prospects. *The Daily Times-Journal* in Fort William lauded the visit as bringing "one step nearer the consummation of plans for marketing the rich hematite ore" and noted that Blackstock had "wide experience in the mining industry and for years has been actively engaged as an executive, director, and officer of numerous important mining companies." At the same time Colonel Blackstock was organizing and managing the Bake-rite Company, of which he was president, (it grew from one store to nine.) He also served as vice-president of the Commercial Lumber Company, and as director of two insurance companies. In 1925 he organized G.G. Blackstock and Company, a member of the Toronto Stock Exchange from 1928 to 1937. He stood (unsuccessfully) in Spadina Riding as a candidate for the non-partisan National Government Party, then became Deputy to Ontario Premier George Drew, where he was responsible for the administration and direction of the business of the premier's offices.

George Blackstock (right) at the Steep Rock Mines, of which he was vice-president.

He made the pages of *Saturday Night*, and that prominent magazine noted that his favourite sports were "golf and badminton, although he does enjoy a ride on a thoroughbred horse or a keen game of indoor baseball."

In 1921 George Blackstock married Bessie Hildegarde Brooke Bell. Toronto's *Globe* extolled the beauty of the bride, in particular her veil with its "orange blossoms and white heather, brought from Scotland." The prominence of the guest list was duly noted — many of whom, family and friends of the Gooderham/Blackstock connection, would, within three years, feel the pressure to put down a pledge and become a founding member of the B&R.

George Blackstock on his wedding day, October 22, 1921.

Originally called Poona, badminton was discovered in India in the 1860s by British soldiers who had seen a local game called "battledore and shuttlecocks" played in the streets. They took the game back to England to the estates of the aristocracy. Rumour had it that the first spirited match was played across a banquet table by army officers using improvised racquets and a bird made of goose quills anchored in a champagne cork. The locale was the estate of the Duke of Beaufort. His property in Gloucester was called Badminton.

British soldiers brought badminton to Vancouver in the 1890s. Countless Canadian soldiers were exposed to the game during World War One as a means to keep fit, and it crossed the Atlantic with vigour to North America at war's end. Clubs were founded, many in army garrisons. Soon 60,000 Canadians were playing the game on an eclectic assortment of court sites. *Maclean's* listed the most innovative locales. The Badminton and Racquet Club made the list.

"In Windsor the Frontier Club was recently inaugurated and a disused market building was transformed into a fine badminton club. In Toronto the Badminton and Racquet Club has utilized a former streetcar barn and is developing players of international caliber. The Carlton Club has turned an old curling rink into a fine court building.... Residents of Arnprior removed pews from a deserted church and laid out two good courts.... A private club purchased an unused aeroplane hanger and brought it to Oakville where it was reassembled to provide the most practical facilities for badminton."

Badminton had rapidly become one of Canada's most popular sports from coast to coast.

With a Few Friends

"We went from one end of the city to the other, and we decided that the old Yorkville Avenue car barns owned by the Toronto and York Radial Railway Company might be converted into a club — they wanted to sell and they wanted cash!"
    Roy Buchanan

"The original membership was to quite an extent composed of married couples, most of whom knew the others already, so mixed doubles in badminton were the order of the day. Most of the members had never tried to hit a bird before, but what they lacked in skill they more than made up in enthusiasm. The game caught on like wildfire…. A few of our best players were invited to the U.S. where it had not yet caught on. Badminton was brand new to we squash players and very fascinating. You had to reserve in person for your weekend game. The 'box office' opened on Thursday morning, so you went in on the way to work to sign up. There was often a long line-up."
    Graeme Watson

"You knew everyone when you went to the club. They were all your friends or friends of your family."
    Miss Geraldine Dack, a university student who played nearly every day with her idols, Esmé Coke and Dorothy Boone

For Male Members
After use, playing clothes should be left or handed to the attendant to be placed in the drying room. They will be placed in lockers when dried and aired. The co-operation of members in this regard is asked as it has been found by experience unless full use of the drying room is made, the lockers and locker room very quickly become foul.
    R.B. Buchanan, Hon. Secretary

It was 1923, and the Canadian Badminton Championships were being held on the courts of the Toronto Garrison Badminton Club on University Avenue. The Canadian Badminton Association had been formed just two years previously in Montreal but there was no lack of devotees. Names that would be on the B&R roster the following year were competing for national titles and organizing the event. Mrs. C.A. Boone was defending her Ladies' Singles Open title, won in the first Canadian championships held in 1922 at the Canadian Army Medical Corps Badminton Club. Dorothy Boone was also competing with her doubles partner, Mrs. Ruggles George, defending their 1922 title. Garrison Club members were on tournament committees. Colonel Blackstock, Roy Buchanan, Murray Garden, J. de N. Kennedy, Mrs. Boone, Mrs. Ruggles George, and Mrs. J. Leys Gooderham were listed. It was from this nucleus of men and women looking for an improvement in playing conditions to share with a few friends, that the Badminton and Racquet Club was founded. The search was on for a club site.

Just at this time the newly formed Toronto Transportation Commission, which had been offering cheerful service since 1921, even on Sunday, had started to amalgamate the various transit systems operating in the Toronto area. It was now transporting the public around the city at an astonishing speed of six miles an hour, with fares collected by the conductor carrying his "coffee pot." Passengers could take the Toronto Railway Company line up Yonge Steet as far as Woodlawn and then, since it was now part of the TTC, transfer to the Toronto and York Radial Railway system. This would take them through the "outer areas," and with countless stops along the way, passengers could travel all the way to Lake Simcoe. With this seemingly vast new system it was time for the TTC to centralize its facilities and get rid of its old car barns and repair shops, now redundant. And so the city empowered the Hydro Electric Power Commission of Ontario, which operated the radial lines, to manage the sales. William Bosley, who had been involved with the real estate interest of the Gooderham family, had been asked by them to keep his eyes open for a site with the necessary ceiling height to accommodate badminton courts. He passed on

The University Avenue Armouries, which housed the Toronto Garrison Badminton Club, home club for George Blackstock and friends prior to the founding of the Badminton and Racquet Club in 1924.

Toronto and York Radial Railway car still owned by Hydro Electric in 1918. Shown at Yonge and Lawton. Christ Church Deer Park in its original location in the background.

Toronto and York Railway, Deer Park Shops, shown circa 1915, as seen from Yonge Street south of St. Clair.

word of the car barns. Enter George Blackstock and Roy Buchanan of the Garrison Club. These old car barns would serve their purpose.

The Metropolitan car barns at the intersection of Yonge and St. Clair, in the Deer Park area, were part of Hydro's sale. The site consisted of three pieces comprising the southwest corner, excluding the Bank of Commerce on the corner itself. And so on April 8, 1924, Colonel Blackstock made an offer to purchase the interior piece, which included 15 feet fronting on St. Clair. (The other two pieces were 245 feet fronting on Yonge Street with a depth of 70 feet, and 187 feet fronting on St. Clair, 180 feet in depth.) The B&R paid $25,000 for their site, $5,000 cash plus a $20,000 mortgage with Hydro. The following month Hydro postponed their $20,000 first mortgage, which then became a second mortgage. The club then arranged a first mortgage, a building loan of $25,000, with the Dominion Life Assurance Company. The access to the B&R's hidden site was that fifteen feet on St. Clair. A wider entrance was needed, and so for $1,000, an additional three-and-a-half feet of frontage was purchased. This gave sufficient access to the club's beleaguered parking lot. Land acquisitions and financing were complete for $51,000. Of this amount $46,000 was in mortgages. Now, how to raise the money? All that was needed was a founding board and some members.

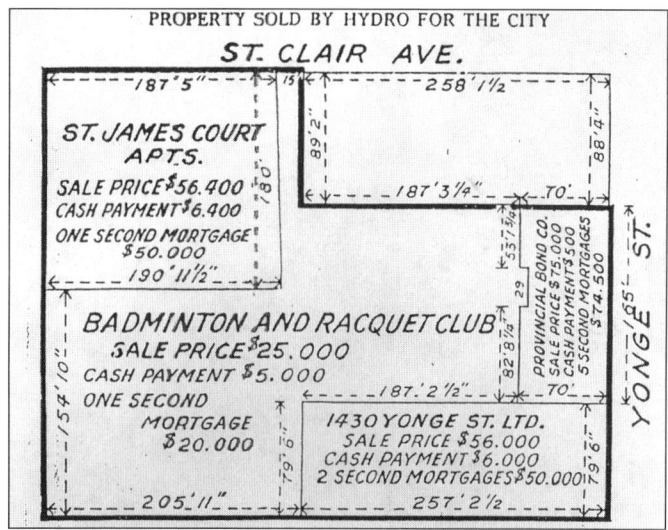

Diagram of the Hydro Electric Power Commission property, showing B&R purchase.

The Letters Patent, May 8, 1924, incorporating the club, listed the first "subscribers," the men who became the club's first directors, as George Gooderham Blackstock, Manufacturer, Charles Lesslie Wilson, Manager of Wilson Publishing Company, William Raymond Thomson, Secretary, Roy Beresford Buchanan, Stockbroker with (J.O.) Buchanan (Norman) Seagram and Co., William Basil Wedd, Vice President and General Manager of Massey Ferguson, and Alexander Murray Garden, Solicitor. (Wedd resigned when his firm moved him to Paris later that year. He was replaced by Harley W. Larkin, President and General Manager, Larkin Lumber.) Blackstock was elected president, Wedd vice-president, and Buchanan honorary secretary. Their purpose as set out was "To promote, organize, conduct, and manage a badminton racquet, squash racquet, tennis, bowling, sports, recreation, and social club and to promote the welfare of the members thereof."

At this point George Blackstock, Roy Buchanan, and the other founding members turned to family and friends, some members of other existing clubs, and cajoled them with sufficient success that by June there were 374 pledges for membership — eight life members at $500, the rest ordinary or non-playing members at $100 or juniors (it was not necessary that a junior be the child of a senior member) at $25. A number of members, many of them women, gave $200, twice the necessary amount, to assist the fledgling project. Annual fees were set at $25. This provided a substantial pledged amount to work with, but Roy Buchanan emphasized that "pledged" was the operative word. Each applicant indicated the sport in which he or she was primarily interested, "badminton or racquets." (All applicants received the unsettling assurance that if their application for membership was turned down their money would be returned.) "That first year was tough," recalled treasurer Buchanan, "but through family arrangements we sold life memberships, mainly to Blackstocks and Gooderhams. We put in a doubles squash racquets court to get the old Toronto Racquet Club (founded in 1905) to come in as members!" The club was proud that, unlike some other

Roy Buchanan, the first Hon. Secretary.

The architect's version of the new Badminton and Racquet Club, a member standing by the elegant circular gardens.

clubs starting up, no commissions were ever paid to those who attracted new members. A founding member said, "We were all friendship and family members."

The firm of George, Moorehouse and King, architects, was brought in. The verdict was that the garage and heating plant with woodworking and repair shop above could be demolished, and a small clubhouse built for $2,450, less than it would cost to re-construct the premises. The car barns could be altered to make seven badminton courts. In the first drawings, featured in the *Hill Rosedale Topics* newsletter, there was, in the centre of the parking lot, a circular island, filled with a cornucopia of plant material and graced by a small fountain. (Perhaps the architects assumed that players would be dropped at the door by a chauffeur who would leave to park elsewhere.) The design also showed a gracious door leading directly from the parking lot to the men's locker room.

By the spring of 1925 construction was complete, without island, fountain, or door. The buildings and furnishings were in place, and all was ready for the grand opening which took place on Saturday, February 7, 1925.

The Globe was there. Most of the guests were the club's original members.

"Nearly 500 guests attended the formal opening of the new Badminton and Racquet Club on Saturday afternoon. The luxuriously furnished lounge overlooking the courts was gaily decorated with spring flowers. An exhibition game was played by George Blackstock, President of the club, Mrs. Charles Boone, Mrs. Coke, and Mr. Kennedy. Among the guests were: Mr. and Mrs. Roy Buchanan, Mr. and Mrs. S. Howard, Mr. and Mrs. James Buchanan, Mr. and Mrs. Carr-Harris, Mr. and Mrs. R.A. Laidlaw, Mr. and Mrs. Douglas Ross, Mrs. E.Y. Eaton, Mr. and Mrs. Christie Clark, Major and Mrs. Charles Boone, Miss Elmsley, Mrs. Hume Wrong, Mr. and Mrs. J.J. Ashworth, Mrs. W. Baldwin, Mr. and Mrs. Graeme Watson, Mrs. G.G. Mitchell, Mrs. T.J. Clarke, Mrs. Eaton Brouse, Mr. and Mrs. Coke, Mr. and Mrs. Eric Armour, Mr. and Mrs. Lesslie Wilson, Mr. and Mrs. Walter Nicholls, Mr. and Mrs. Carpenter, Reginald Parmenter, Dr. and Mrs. Ruggles George, Mr. and Mrs. Leys Gooderham, Lt.Colonel and Mrs. Langford, Major and Mrs. Baxter, Mrs. Torrance Beardmore, Mr. and Mrs. Huntley Christie, Mrs. Campbell Reaves, Mrs. Leslie Martin, Mrs. George Evans, Misses Nanton, Mr. and Mrs. George Magann, Mr. and Mrs. Savage, Gerald Larkin, Mr. and Mrs. Harold Larkin, Mr. and Mrs. Cecil Lee, Miss Suckling, Mrs. George Kingstone, Mrs. Douglas Mason, Mr. and Mrs. Crowther, Miss Crowther, Miss Isobel Cawthra, Miss Pipon, Mr. and Mrs. R.C. Brown, Miss Margaret Walsh, Mrs. James Edgar, Miss Grace Edgar, Mr. and Mrs. George Evans, Mr. and Mrs. Murray Garden, Mr. and Mrs. Albert Poupore, Madam Panet, Mrs. Edgar Jarvis, Mrs. McWhinney, Mr. and Mrs. Birks, Mrs. James White, Mrs. W. Gooderham, the Misses Gooderham, and Mr. and Mrs. A.H.C. Proctor."

The lounge and dining area of the original club, now the Blackstock Room.

The Badminton Hall, formerly the car barns.

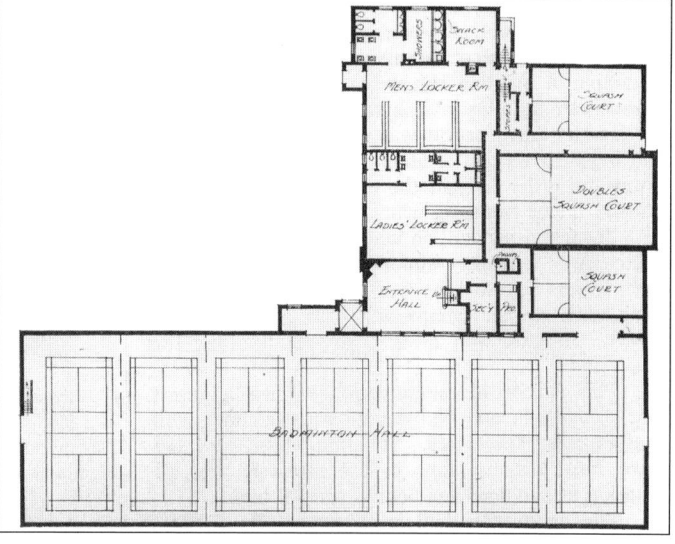

The ground floor plan of the Badminton and Racquet Club.

The entrance hall, stairs as today. A left turn at the top took you to the dining/lounge area.

The Lounge.

Progress views during work.

An Explosion of Membership and Courts Full of Champions

"The curtains were seldom drawn across the big windows in the entrance hall. There were eager members sitting on benches watching the badminton games and waiting their turn to play…. The [second floor] lounge faced on the badminton courts as well and through its windows one could sit and watch the games being played below…. You had to book a court well ahead and only for half an hour at a time. You were not at all popular if you tried to hold a court for two consecutive half hours."

Olive Gooderham

"It was cold in the badminton hall, but we took that for granted. As students we wore shorts, as seniors sleeveless dresses."

Marion Armstrong

"The first time I played badminton at the B&R they had a pot-bellied stove in the corner of the car barns — the place had just been bought."

Paul Flemming

"Mrs. Coke and Mrs. Boone didn't play with you, you played with them."

Ann Blaikie, the club's first junior ladies' badminton champion.

By November 1924 the number of members had leapt from the original 374 to 538. By the spring of 1925 the board's proposed cap of 750 had nearly been met. Everything was heading up, including expenses and fees. The entrance fee was on a climb, to $150 in November, $200 in January and $300 shortly after that. The balance sheet for 1925 showed money spent for "Land and buildings at cost plus furniture and equipment at cost $130,159.82." By this time $77,000 had been gathered in entrance fees. With mortgages for $46,000, plus cash and inventory, this balanced the books. Also on a roll was the waiting list for membership. The B&R was becoming *the* place to play.

The club had found its first pro, O.E. (Tim) Gray, an American who was an outstanding teacher and player. He excelled at squash and tennis but no sooner had he settled in than Mrs. E.F. (Esmé) Coke, member and Canadian champion who played badminton with extraordinary style

Membership form, 1924.

and finesse, took him in hand. He became adept at the game and encouraged the juniors. Marion Armstrong, who joined in 1925, remembers that he cheerfully and informally helped her and her friends when they came over to the club after school. Tim went to Cape Cod in the summer as a pro (in early days the B&R was not open all year, closing from April to October) until the club gave him a full-time contract. His assistant was Gordon Cook, badminton pro, who later went as a professional to the Carlton Club and then to Montreal. Tim and Gordon were on salary. Court fees, a charge of twenty-five cents per half hour, were to cover that cost. The financial arrangements were later changed to give the pro a full percentage on supplies and the whole of the fees from lessons to members.

To promote sales Tim had a popular gimmick. When a member he knew well came in to buy a new racquet — most members changed their wooden racquets each year — he would flip them for double or nothing. Gray went to the Cricket Club two mornings and one afternoon per week. Initially the B&R received half his remuneration. This was changed in 1930, allowing him to keep all of those extra earnings.

And Tim Gray earned his salary. He gave lessons, looked after bookings, sold supplies, collected all the chits for courts, and sought a balance at day's end between chits and courts used. This was all in addition to a variety of duties, a job description set out by the House Committee. He was "responsible for the cleanliness of the Men's Locker Room, Squash Courts, Passageways, and Badminton Courts and will make inspection of the Locker Room by 10:00 A.M. daily and at three hour periods to ensure that it is kept in orderly condition. Professional is responsible for the heating of the building and for the hot water until six P.M. when this duty will be taken over by the Caretaker." He stayed for 20 years, resigning in 1946 to join his brother in the U.S.

Tim Gray worked extremely well with a man who became one of the B&R's well-known institutions. David Russell was the first man on staff with the job of arranging matches for members. And he did this in more than one way. He made introductions. If a junior was looking discreetly around when he or she came in the door David would help the romance along by calling out, "Look on

"Everyone had a bottle of hooch in his locker — we got warning when there was going to be a raid and so we were all clean when the local constabulary arrived."
Anonymous

court three!" He took pride in the number of permanent matches for which he felt he was responsible.

By far the majority of the club's first members were badminton players. It was estimated that 225 played badminton in a ten-hour day. That was one-third of the membership on the courts on a daily basis. There was so much action on the seven badminton courts — three that could be reserved and four open — that a sign-up board had to be put in place for open courts. Otherwise the waiting crowds at the back of the courts overwhelmed the players. The purchase of nearly 6,000 shuttles in 1927 shows the action.

The B&R quickly became known as a training ground and home base for national badminton champions. Mrs. E.F. (Esmé) Coke won the Canadian Ladies' Singles title five times and the doubles four with Mrs. C.A. (Dorothy) Boone. Dorothy Boone won the Canadian Ladies' Singles once, and the doubles five years in a row, twice with Mrs. Ruggles George in addition to the four wins with Esmé Coke. Canadian Men's Doubles titles were captured by George Blackstock and Cyril K.F. Andrewes in 1928, 1930, and 1931. Jack Taylor, football star of the Toronto Argos and the Varsity Blues, won the Canadian Men's Singles in 1931. Esmé Coke and John de N Kennedy won the Mixed Doubles title in 1925. The event was held at the B&R.

Part of badminton's intense popularity was that matches between national champions could be seen any day of the week with the club's own stars. The club championships for 1925-1926 were won by:

Men's Singles	G.G. Blackstock
Ladies' Singles	Mrs. E. F. Coke
Men's Doubles	G.G. Blackstock
	J. de N. Kennedy
Ladies' Doubles	Mrs. C.A. Boone
	Mrs. E.F. Coke
Mixed Doubles	Mrs. E.F. Coke
	G.G. Blackstock

All were or would soon be Canadian champions, and they were available for play with eager juniors!

Dorothy L. Boone
Badminton

Canadian Open
Ladies Singles
1922

Canadian Ladies
Doubles
1922, 1923, 1924,
1925, 1926, 1928

Esmé F. Coke
Badminton

Canadian Ladies
Singles
1924, 1925, 1926,
1928, 1929

Canadian Ladies
Doubles
1924, 1925, 1926,
1928

Canadian Mixed
Doubles
1925

Note to all junior members, December, 1926.

TO ALL JUNIOR MEMBERS   December 8, 1926.

In order to stimulate interest in Badminton amongst the Junior Members, the Courts Committee have arranged that two Courts will be reserved every Saturday morning from 9.30 a.m. until noon for the use of Junior members only.

Shuttles may be had free of charge from the Professional.

Mrs. E.F. Coke and several lady players have kindly consented to act as instructors and play with Juniors during this period.

The Committee hopes that Junior Members will avail themselves of this opportunity to improve their game, as it is intended to hold Junior championships towards the end of the season.

FOR THE COURTS COMMITTEE
A. Murray Garden
Captain.

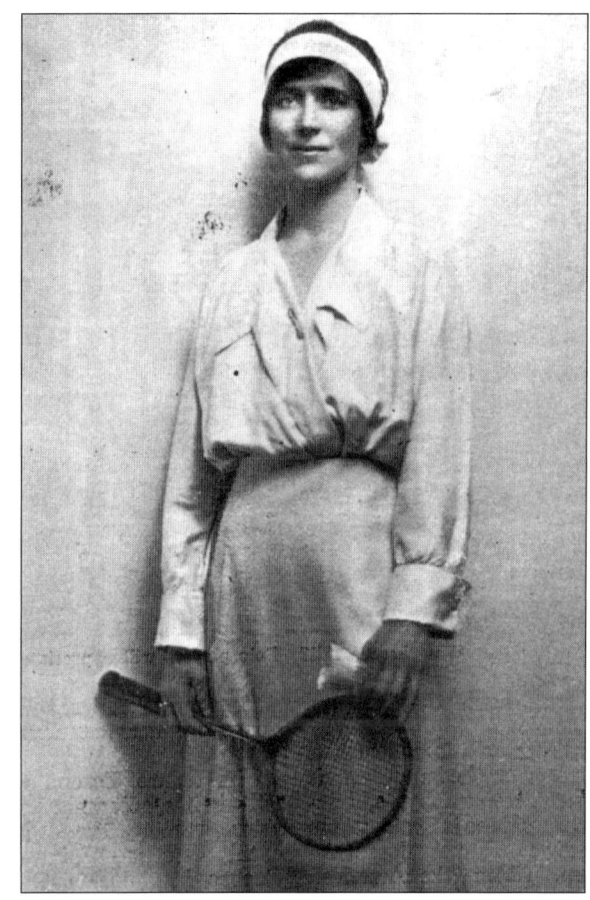

Cherith Esmé Coke was born in 1899 in St. Helens, England. She came to Canada in 1920 as a war bride, having met her Canadian husband on a British tennis court, (he had lived in Winnipeg prior to the war and had gone overseas with the Fort Garry Horse.) Esmé was first of all a tennis player, and did not play badminton until she moved to Winnipeg. The Cokes relocated to Toronto in 1922 and Esmé played badminton at the Armories. Four years after she first held a badminton racquet she became Canadian Singles champion. That was 1924, and she repeated her Canadian title in 1925, 1926, (her daughter, Cherith, was born in 1927,) 1928, and 1929. At the time of the 1928 competitions she was six months pregnant, which clearly did nothing to slow her down. The *Mail and Empire* proclaimed that she "practically dominated the competition throughout." With her partners she won four Canadian doubles titles and one Canadian mixed doubles title.

Esmé went to England in 1930 to play in the All-England tournament, won the pre-tournament, but injured her arm in the process and never won a tournament again. She played her last badminton match in the Ontario championships, which were held at the B&R in 1951. She was suffering from cancer but still playing on. When she appeared, one admiring spectator exclaimed, "You have to watch Mrs. Coke, she has been playing for a hundred years." Esmé Coke was made the first life member of the club for her significant contributions.

In his report to the club's second annual meeting, in 1926, an exuberant George Blackstock lauded the new club's reputation for national champions, so quickly established. In City, Ontario and Canadian championships the "Club entered twelve of the fifteen events played in these three championships, and thanks mainly to the ladies,

Cyril K. F. Andrewes
Tennis

Member Canadian
Davis Cup Team
1924

Badminton
Canadian Men's
Doubles
1928, 1930, 1931

George G. Blackstock
Badminton

Canadian Men's
Doubles
1928, 1930, 1931

Cyril Andrewes was born in 1883 in England and attended Harrow School, where he showed a natural aptitude for all racquet sports. He became Public Schools Rackets Champion. Rackets is an extremely fast game involving a hard ball; it was the forerunner of squash. At Cambridge he obtained his Blue in tennis and field hockey and his Cap for England in an international match. Invited to play on the Davis Cup team for England, he declined in order to travel, and in those travels he entered tennis tournaments wherever he happened to be. He won the New Jersey State Men's Singles, the Jamaica Men's Singles, the Barbados Men's Singles and, with Scott Griffin, the Manitoba Men's Open Doubles. He reached the semifinals of the U.S. Championships. After serving in the war, Cyril and his wife, the daughter of railroad magnate Sir William MacKenzie, moved to Toronto where he became a founding member of the B&R and, with George Blackstock, winner of the Canadian Doubles Championships from 1928 to 1931. He played on Canada's Davis Cup team in 1924 at the age of 41. He never lost interest in racquet sports and followed their explosive growth until his death at age 95.

Blackstock and Andrewes.

won nine finals and was represented in the finals of the other three."

If, however, the membership was becoming overconfident, that euphoric feeling was temporarily dispelled when Sir George Thomas, Baronet, brought six of the highest ranking badminton players in the world, the English International Badminton Team, to Canada and the B&R on December 9, 1925. The club spared no expense for the occasion — $2,041 covered meals and shuttles, matting, platforms, chairs, and ushers. So popular was the event, however, that ticket sales covered the cost. Eleven matches were played, mainly doubles, with one mixed doubles set

Cartoon of Cyril Andrewes.

The operations of the club are divided into three departments, the General, which absorbs the general expenses of the Club, such fixed charges as heat, light, office expenses, caretaking etc. and depreciation on buildings and furnishings. These expenses are met from annual fees and locker rentals. General expenses during the year exceeded revenue by $2,672.51 The second department, the Courts, is intended to carry itself, with the revenue from Court Fees, visitors' fees, profit on shuttles and tournaments meeting the Professional's salary and general expenses of up-keep. During the year the Courts department showed a profit of $307.14 The third department, the House, is also intended as far as possible to carry itself from the revenue from meals, cigarettes, etc. During the year the House showed a loss of $638.15. The total deficit for the year is therefore $3,003.52. We cannot run the club on annual fees of $25 per year, but we believe we can assure you that we can for $30.

Annual Report, 1926, George Blackstock

in which Esmé Coke and Dorothy Boone participated. Graeme Watson recalled the day. "We invited a group of Englishmen over as our guests. We thought that they looked like old codgers — they were probably 50 — but they had Blackstock and Andrewes running all over the courts like rabbits to keep up with their well placed shots."

The club hosted many tournaments during these early years, including the Dominion Badminton championships, which it shared with Vancouver and Winnipeg, hosting the event every third year, as well as the first Ontario badminton championships in 1925. Indeed, 1925 was a prestigious year for the B&R. The club was chosen as the site of the founding meeting of the Ontario Badminton Association (OBA). Roy Buchanan was elected vice-president, to act with the president, Colonel A.E. Snell of Ottawa. George Blackstock

> "I joined in 1927 as a junior in my teens. My parents joined many years later. I came in on my own. Bud Southam was my great friend and contemporary there. Ed Deeks was a big fellow whose father was the head of Abitibi. Ed had a great eye. He moved around slowly on the badminton court but in doubles he was a great asset. I played with Peter and Bill Boulton, of the old Boulton family of The Grange, Ronald Sniffen, and John Gilmour who lived on Bedford Road. John's family had a house in Oakville. I used to stay there when the B&R played the Oakville Club in the badminton league. We played home and home games with the Granite Club, the Boulevard Club, the York Club, but the best one of the year was the annual visit to the Oakville Club by the river."
>
> *Frank Lace*

Tennis in 1929. Left to right: Mildred Brock, Esmé Coke, Rayne Macdonnell, Vi Parker.

became honorary secretary. Roy Buchanan was president of the OBA from 1927 to 1929. George Blackstock held that office from 1929 to 1932. And from 1955 to 1957 Bev Westcott brought the presidency back to the B&R.

Members were soon on the road or hosting interclub badminton matches, pitting their talents against clubs in Guelph, Oakville, London, Kingston, St. Catharines and Oshawa, and clubs in Montreal and Quebec City. Stalwart B&R pairs took on Hamilton and Buffalo in one day. An invitation was received by B&R men to visit various locations in New York State to introduce or encourage the game there. Badminton was known to be played just as extensively in Canada as in England, and the prowess of the club's stars had spread. This tour was a great compliment since New York boasted the old New York City Badminton Club, established in 1878, with a membership of only 200, and a waiting list as long as the entire membership list. Only single young men or women were eligible to be proposed for membership, and it was tense when you found yourself on the brink of matrimony and still not elected.

John S. Proctor
Tennis

Canadian Open
Men's Doubles
1926
Canadian Mixed
Doubles
1925, 1930

Once again George Blackstock could boast of the members' achievements, this time claiming victories gained by sending the second string against the others' best. "During the year [1926] the Club played eighteen inter-club matches, winning all but three. In no case was the Club represented by its full playing strength, but rather by a team which would be representative of the average play in the club, and at the same time be sufficiently strong to win, or at least give a good account of itself."

Tickets for travelling B&R pairs were booked and hotel accommodation arranged by the club. The teams consisted of "twelve ladies and twelve men which will allow six matches in ladies' and men's doubles and twelve in mixed doubles." These matches were weekly events, at home or away, every Saturday night from November to March, and were usually followed by an evening of dinner and dancing. Members were urged to practise, to be alert and aggressive and "assume the offensive as quickly as possible." They were advised that, "a good general definition of being on the offensive is when you are hitting the shuttle down and your opponents are returning by hitting up.... [N]o opportunity should ever be missed to deal severely with a badly hit shuttle...a high serve, unless well back of the court, should be punished. Such treatment has a most disturbing effect and creates nervousness in the server."

The club's three squash courts — two singles and one doubles — were situated on the east side of the clubhouse.

NOTICE

CLUB BLAZER

Your Committee have approved of the style of the Club blazer for the use of all members of the Club.

This blazer is of white flannel with a maroon and white ribbon, and the Club crest worked in maroon on the pocket.

Messrs. Beauchamp & How Co., 91 King Street West, have the ribbon and are in a position to make these for members. The price of the blazer is $16.50

Ladies who may wish to have these made by their own tailors may secure a crest and the necessary ribbon from the Secretary.

It is hoped that these will be extensively used by the membership of the Club.

Brown, Secretary.

Notice re: club blazer.

They were part of the original construction, and the doubles squash court was, according to charter member Ramsey Fraser, the "first and only" doubles court in Ontario. (It had been installed initially in an effort to recruit squash players from The University Club and The Toronto Racquet Club.) The popularity of the squash ball, however, didn't initially rival the popularity of the badminton bird. As Arthur Bishop put it in *The First Fifty*, "Squash was simply a pumpkin-like vegetable as far as most members were concerned."

John H. Chipman
Squash

Canadian Men's Amateur Singles
1926

Out of town visitors (20 miles from the city) may be introduced by a member for a period of two weeks, on a charge of fifty cents for each day the courts are used.
*Board Minutes,
January 30, 1925*

The official club crest has been sketched by J. Scott Carter
*Board Minutes,
November 24, 1926*

But if the doubles squash court did not receive enough play, there was another use discovered by an innovative couple after a club dance. The incident was related by Ramsey Fraser:

"Some mean-spirited member happened to notice a prominent B&R female member enter the darkened doubles squash court with a male competitor from the West Coast. [The member] raced upstairs and assembled an audience at the blackened window in the dining lounge. [There was a viewing window from the combination dining room and lounge area from which a few spectators would gather to watch squash.] A zealous accomplice with his hand on the light switch awaited the signal. What a scene unfolded before the multitude behind the viewing window! It quickly dispelled the old Kipling adage of East meeting West and never twaining. And it did give the doubles court some usage, albeit from the badminton section." The doubles court was closed in 1936, from lack of much use other than for romantic assignations. The club did not have a doubles squash court again until 1957.

Tennis received its first mention in 1925, when a discussion took place about draining and levelling the marshalling yards to make four clay courts. The expenses would be covered by the tennis fee, which was increased to $5 for a senior member, $2 for a junior. The question of keeping the club open in the summer came up, a dramatic change from its early days as a winter facility only. It was decided that a trial would take place "to endeavour to create sufficient interest in tennis." Ladies' and men's locker rooms would be open, but no refreshments or cigarettes would be available. In 1927 the tennis committee announced that "the Tennis Courts are now being played on. It is hoped that they will be well patronized and sufficient interest taken to warrant tournaments being played." As an inducement the committee arranged with Hunt's Catering Service "that cold drinks, afternoon teas, and light meals may be served in the Club premises."

No opportunity for socializing was ever lost. In addition to the Saturday night mixed interclub matches and dances, there were many special highlights. A gala event

Arthur W. Ham
Tennis

Member Canadian
Davis Cup Team
1926, 1927,
1928, 1929

"Tim Gray was a really good badminton player and a marvelous pro. He sparked a lot of us and got us going. I think that badminton is the toughest racquet game, tougher than squash and tennis. The birds seemed very expensive then, and they seemed to break easily. I was playing with broken birds a lot of the time. The birds were made of feathers, cork, and a bit of real leather, hand-made. And the racquets were relatively expensive. They were hand-strung. I was given one to start and it broke so I bound it up with metal and fixed it for play."

Frank Lace

"The Bal Masque was a wow....the badminton floor was used for dancing ... the orchestra was on a platform at the east end under the clock. The walls were all decorated with flags and bunting ... and an occasional oyster patty or a few designs in gravy." Various costumes were, "an Upper Canada College Prep boy, a sailor, Rob Roy, a badminton shuttle, a pullman porter, a bookie with brown check suit and bowler, a butterfly, a convict." H. Brooke Bell, a board member, is far left, and Nan McCarthy, his future wife, second from the left, back row.
From a letter, April, 1927, H. Brooke Bell to Bessie Blackstock.

was made out of the provincial elections in 1926. Notices explained that arrangements had been made with the Canadian National Telegraph Company for receiving election returns. "A special wire will be installed; an operator engaged and returns will be announced and recorded promptly." A special dinner was served for $1.50 and members could extend the privileges of the club to guests for the occasion. Another memorable event was the fancy dress ball held on April 1, 1927. Nobody was admitted to the club if not in costume. A buffet dinner was served at seven-thirty. The cost of the evening was $3.50.

In the first decade, traditions were being established. There were complaints to the board — the court fees, chits payable for each half hour, were extremely unpopular! There was no heating in the badminton hall; the glass roof reflected too much light. The board issued a statement gently chastising the members:

"It was easier to get into the Granite Club in those days than to get into the B&R. You wouldn't want to join the Badminton and Racquet Club if you didn't play badminton, squash, or tennis. In the beginning it was an athletic club where everybody played."

It was agreed to allow the House Committee to make a service charge of twenty-five cents on all dinners served after 8 p.m.
Board Minutes, November 26, 1927

The captain of the junior boys will be Mr. Trevor Manning. The captain of the junior girls will be Mrs. J.C. Suydam. Junior membership will begin at age 15.
Board Minutes, January, 1928

New china with the club crest has been purchased for $600.
Board Minutes, March 8, 1929

It is agreed to set aside $250 a year for the purchase of pictures.
Board Minutes, October 21, 1929

"I went on a West Indies cruise and met a charming couple named Dupont. When they heard that I was a Canadian they knew at once that I was a badminton player. When they learned that I was a member of the Badminton and Racquet Club they said I must be the best badminton player they had ever met in their lives. They had their own badminton court in Wilmington, Delaware, and invited me to visit and play there. Three of their friends had their own badminton courts as well, and I was delegated to spend five days playing badminton in Wilmington. I had the run of the whole city as their guest because I was a Canadian and, the ultimate, a member of the B&R."

In the early 1920s and 30s this was first and foremost a badminton club. Interclub competition was great and we all competed on the club's A and B teams. The interclub spirit was great in those days. We had a knock rummy competition with the Carlton Club, home and home games. It was purely stag and what a time we had. Dominoes started right away as a major sport. I remember Jakey Jackson. He was one of the best."

I remember playing in a competition with Esmé Coke. We were sent to Ottawa. Then the great teams were playing up and back, but she had only played sides. She insisted on playing that way but said she would make a deal. If she couldn't hold up her end she would play net. We met Margaret Robertson and Bev Mitchell and they drove the bird right through her. She came to me and said she would go to the net. She had never played net before but that day she played the most magnificent net game I have ever seen."

Members recollecting the early days at the time of the fiftieth anniversary, in 1974.

It is of interest to record that the Club is unique we believe, in the world, as the only Club which has constructed a hall to house the badminton courts, consequently many points of construction and operation affecting such things as lighting, both artificial and daylight, background, flooring, method of charging for shuttles, engaging of courts, etc, were decided only after the most careful consideration, but without previous experience to guide us.

The members in turn chastised the board by roundly defeating their by-law change allowing five day members. The courts were too crowded already, the members said, and don't make by-law changes without coming to the membership. Thus started a tradition of a feisty and never complacent membership.

Just before the end of the decade, four years after the opening of the club, the first "improvements" were suggested. There would be $3,200 spent on the kitchen, the ladies' locker room would be enlarged, and changes made in the badminton hall, a seventy-foot- long gallery and large glass windows for viewing the courts, a total of $16,000 would be spent. The tradition of "improvements" had been established. It would stand the test of time, making the club's facilities a work in progress!

The Thirties

"The doubles squash court was used so little it was converted to another purpose in the first re-arrangement of the premises. One singles court was more than enough. The other was used for storage, and so that's where Christie Clark and I put a Ping-Pong table."
    Graeme Watson

NOTICE
Lady Members are requested to be more careful when parking cars, and to park close together on the sides before using the centre!
    Arthur Brown,
      Secretary, November, 1937

"There was a singles squash court that we finally made into a locker room, but kids kept coming in. We men couldn't be alone. I was president at the time [1938] and I decided we didn't need that locker room. I thought it might be a good idea to cut the locker room in half and make half of it an older men's lounge. So during the summer I cut it in half and it was made over. I gave all the pictures and some furniture. I had no authorization by the board or from anybody. We had a stodgy board member who came back in the fall and asked what had happened. I told him I had cut the locker in half. 'Who authorized that?' he asked. 'Nobody,' was my answer. 'No board meeting?' he said. 'No,' said I. 'Goodbye,' he said. 'Goodbye,' said I. And for years it was known as Duggan's Room, the senior men's room."
    Mike Duggan,
      at the club's fiftieth anniversary.

The question of allowing members to wear shorts on the Badminton Courts was discussed and the recommendation from the Courts Committee to allow this was accepted.
    Board Minutes, January 15, 1932

The House Committee has requested that no canned sausages or canned mushrooms be used.
    Board Minutes, November 29, 1934

The thirties began with the ladies being heard from in several areas. Women had been full members since the club was founded. Their numbers almost equalled those of the men, and they paid the same fees. There had been a ladies' committee since 1927. Its role, as the committee and the board saw it, was to be responsible "for purely ladies' social events; playing events such as round robins; to help entertain visiting teams and care for visiting lady players; to give advice to the General Committee when approached re lady members of House or Badminton Committees." But their voices were not being heard except in these housekeeping and entertaining roles. And so, perhaps spurred on by the fact that they had just achieved one concession from the board when the telephone line was extended into their locker rooms, they courageously voiced two complaints.

The first complaint was that the board *was* the membership committee. New members applications were not voted on by the current membership, but by the board. (Only four board members voted, and one blackball was sufficient to deny membership.) The women brought the matter to the board's attention and suggested that membership admission be by a full vote. This was refused.

Then, undeterred, on the tenth anniversary of the club's inception, the lady members stepped boldly into an area that would be a subject of heated debate for nearly fifty years. They suggested that while women were represented on the house and badminton committees, they should have representation on the board of directors, as well. The board's absolute refusal came in a letter from President Norman Seagram to Mrs. C. Lesslie Wilson of

> **THE BADMINTON AND RACQUET CLUB**
> *of* TORONTO
>
> December 19th, 1930
>
> At the request of many Members the Directors have agreed to open a Fund on New Year's Day for the relief of unemployed.
>
> Members can make donations direct to the Secretary or deposit their contribution in a receptacle provided for that purpose at the New Year's Day luncheon.
>
> A contribution of One Dollar per Member will be most acceptable.

the ladies' committee. The explanation was simple. "Many men of the type we want cannot be persuaded to go on the Directorate and as to those who have, a great deal of persuasion had to be used before getting their consent.... I am satisfied in my own mind that if the By-Laws are amended to include women on the Directorate, it is going to become increasingly difficult to persuade desirable men to stand for election. " After this classic explanation the president agreed that the men's committee would meet with the ladies' committee to discuss their concerns. The response was a thank-you for this "generous letter." The matter was put to sleep for a while!

There was one area, however, in which lady members were extended privileges very unusual for the time. Lady members "in business" were extended the same playing privileges as men. They could arrange doubles badminton games on Saturday afternoons, Sundays, and from 5 to 7 p.m. on week-days, times not available to the regular lady members.

"One woman was proposed for membership and all the names on her application were those of men. That caused a bit of a stir in those days."
Barbara Proctor

John M. Taylor
Badminton

Canadian Men's
Singles
1931

Walter M. Martin
Tennis

Member
Canadian Davis
Cup Team
1931, 1932,
1933, 1934

Canadian Open
Men's Doubles
1937

Meanwhile the club's badminton players were still travelling, taking the B&R's reputation across Canada. When in 1931 young Jack Taylor won the Canadian Men's Singles Badminton Championship, his name joined the club's prestigious list of champions. A well-known Toronto Argo backfield ace, Taylor was proclaimed as "fleet of foot and as brilliant on the badminton court as on a rugby gridiron" and "a dashing figure who has thrilled thousands of rugby fans through his sensational form in broken field running…. The Torontonian made few mistakes, while his footwork was a treat to the gallery. Aspiring players can do no better than observe this truly great player in action." *The Bridle and Golfer* described his prowess: "He started playing badminton a little over four years ago and celebrated his twenty-first birthday last month. In the Badminton and

NOTICE
December 3rd, 1937.

The attention of the lady members is called to their dress when playing Badminton. White should be worn as far as possible.

A white "sports" costume with regulation white flannel Badminton shorts is preferable to the "Beach" type of diminutive shorts and those of varied colours.

For the Ladies' Committee,

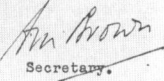
Secretary.

25 ST. CLAIR AVENUE WEST
TORONTO 5

March 12th, 1932

A HARD-TIMES PARTY

will be held at the Club on

April Fools' Day, Friday, April 1st

for Members and <u>their Guests</u>

A Buffet Dinner will be served at 8.30 p.m.

Dancing in the Badminton Courts from 9 till 2.

Supper at midnight.

Music will be furnished by Stanley St. John and his twelve-piece orchestra.

Reservations should be made with the Secretary or on the notice card in the Club as soon as possible, as only a limited number of tickets will be sold.

Admission will be by ticket only.

Double ticket $5.00.   Single ticket $3.00.

Dress as you please.   Special Attractions.

Jack Taylor, in 1931, on the occasion of winning the Canadian Men's Singles Badminton championship.

Racquet Club of Toronto he has been quite a factor, winning first the junior championship and last year the senior… His all round strength is primarily responsible for his success."

Money was generally extended for travel expenses to players entering Canadian and Ontario championships. Esmé Coke had made trips to Vancouver as well as various locations in Ontario. Jack Taylor was assisted with his next trip to Vancouver for the Canadian championships. In 1932 grants were made to the club's participants in the Canadians in Winnipeg — C.K.F Andrewes, J.M. Taylor, H.A. Henderson, and R.B. Buchanan. The sum of $125 was given to a team of ladies to play badminton in Ottawa for the Hodgson Trophy.

No grants were given, however, to players attending the Canadian Squash Championships in Ottawa. The matter would be reviewed, as the board tactfully put it, "whenever any players showed championship form." Interest in squash had yet to take off. As Peter Watson noted recently in his article *Squash Walls of Fame*, a summary of squash at the B&R, "When the Club was established in 1924 … there were two singles and one doubles squash court along the east wall of the ground floor. It was the only doubles court in Toronto.

In 1936 the original doubles squash court was closed, and three new singles squash courts were built at the south end of the building. The former squash area was converted into locker rooms and general use rooms and became the home of the "back room boys."

The new squash courts (and the prowess of the club's lady members) made the pages of the *Globe and Mail* in December 1936. The praise was effusive:

Gilbert Nunns
Tennis

Member of the
Canadian Davis
Cup Team
1927, 1928, 1930,
1931, 1932, 1933,
1934

Canadian Open
Men's Doubles
1937

Canadian Junior
Men's Singles
1924, 1925

Inducted into the
Canadian Tennis
Hall of Fame
1993

Hope H. Salmond
Tennis

Canadian Open
Ladies Doubles
1932

Ruby Fisher
Tennis

Canadian Open
Ladies Doubles
1938, 1948

John K. McCausland
Squash

Canadian Men's
Doubles
1934

"Racquet Stars to Meet Today
The Badminton and Racquet Club of Toronto has a thousand active members including fifty or sixty juniors, which is the largest membership in Toronto. The women players collectively are the best in the city. [The York Badminton Club, the paper allowed, had the strongest men.].... Mr. Tim Gray is the instructor.... Recently [the club] acquired three new squash courts that Mr. Gray believes are the best in Canada. The club is open afternoons and evenings seven days a week. The largest crowd appears on Sundays.... The Badminton and Racquet Club of Toronto will hold their first skating party on Monday evening on their flooded tennis courts." (For many years, before the club had Har-Tru courts, the original hard surface was flooded to provide a skating rink.)

BADMINTON & RACQUET CLUB
NOTICE TO MEMBERS

CHRISTMAS DANCE
 An Annual Xmas Dance will be held at the Club on Tuesday, December 25th and will be open to Members, both Senior and Junior, and their guests. Reservations for this event should be made with the Secretary's office before December 20th. Tickets $1.50 per person.

NEW YEAR'S LUNCHEON
 A Special Buffet Luncheon will be served on New Year's Day from 12.30 p.m. to 3.30 p.m. for which a nominal charge of $1.00 per person will be charged to defray out-of-pocket expenses. Owing to the limited facilities of the Club house, Members are requested to refrain from inviting guests to this Luncheon.

For the House Committee
W. L. KIRBY, *Secretary*

The new squash courts received further praise when the Toronto City Squash Racquets Championships were held at the B&R. "The new courts of the Badminton and Racquet Club have been designed with the purpose of giving spectators a much better view of the play than heretofore. Jack McCausland of the Badminton and Racquet Club is defending his title for the Chipman Cup." (This cup, for T&D singles squash, was given by John H. "Jack" Chipman, winner of the Canadian Men's Singles Squash title in 1926 and later a member of the B&R.)

But while the B&R continued to receive great press coverage for its facilities and for the prowess of its members, a dissenting voice up the street was capturing press attention as well. At the corner of Heath and Yonge streets, Canon Woodcock, Rector of Christ Church Deer Park, had just learned that the B&R was advertising round robins on Sunday mornings from 10:15 to 12:30. The following Sunday he preached on the subject, reading the club's notice from the pulpit. He went on to proclaim, "That club whose members comprise leaders in Toronto's social and industrial and commercial life, has authorized an organized effort to stimulate the interest of its members in a badminton round robin at the very hour when the bells of every church in this city are calling people to prayer and worship." Warming to his subject, he linked the round robins to a general decline in the morals of the community. It is not clear what effect this sermon had on the round

CANADIAN BADMINTON CHAMPIONSHIPS

Will be held on
March 1st, 2nd and 3rd, 1934

Under the auspices of the
ONTARIO BADMINTON ASSOCIATION

On the Courts of the
BADMINTON AND RACQUET CLUB
OF TORONTO

25 St. Clair Avenue West
Toronto, Ontario

Tournament Committee
A. E. HOLLINGS (Chairman)
C. K. F. ANDREWES
PROF. C. W. ARGUE
G. S. H. COOK
P. J. HANLEY
W. N. KEENAN
PROF. W. L. MALCOLM
J. C. SUYDAM

Tournament Secretary
B. B. BUCHANAN

Referee
LT.- COL. G. G. BLACKSTOCK

TORONTO CENTENNIAL 1834-1934

"My family weren't members but this was not unusual. There were lots of juniors who had no family connections, yet everyone knew who you were. The best players were very good with the juniors — Mrs. Coke, Mrs. Boone, Mrs. Gardiner, Mrs. Olive Gooderham. Mrs. Boone was marvellous, a large, jolly woman with slender legs. She could cover the whole court. As a junior you had to wait for an empty court and if any seniors wanted a court you had to get off. If seniors were short a player they would ask us to join them, but they made us behave. There were wonderful round robins. Tim Gray had a little office overlooking the badminton courts and he might put his head out and tell you that your serve wasn't right. He could see everything. If you were short a player, he would come out and play."
Barbara Proctor

robins or the attendance of B&R members, many of whom were his parishioners.

The good canon would have been further convinced that morals in the St. Clair and Yonge area were in jeopardy had he known that one member of the B&R had just been chastised for having his bootlegger deliver liquor to him at the club on a Sunday, or that two members had been suspended for forcing entry into the club in the early hours of a Sunday morning "in the company of two young ladies."

But the legitimate social life at the club was booming, with the Saturday night dinners and dances the

> It has been suggested that the tennis courts be flooded to use for skating and that they be lit at night. It is to be hoped that this will increase dining along with skating.
> *Annual Meeting, 1935*

favourite. The dining room menu was set at one dollar (a "plate dinner" could be obtained for seventy-five cents), and the orchestra was always a huge success. In fact, so popular were these dances that it was decided more supervision was needed and so two board members had to stay with the party until lights out at 2:30 a.m. Imagination knew no bounds when special dances were planned. Paul Flemming told of one, which he called the most successful ever held, to which every member went dressed as the opposite sex. "I went as a Salvation Army lass," he related at the time of the fiftieth anniversary dinner, "and called on Mrs. Manning, Trevor's mother, with my tambourine. She gave me fifty cents."

But the most lavish ball of all was held on April 23, 1937. It was the Coronation Ball and Dinner, marking the coronation of King George VI. Stanley St. John's fifteen-piece orchestra was engaged to play for dancing from 9:00 p.m. until 3:00 a.m., with a dinner from 8:00 to 9:00 p.m. (price $1.00) and a buffet supper from 12:30 until 2:00 a.m. Cars could be parked at the nearby Granite Club for 25¢ per car. The club spent $2,100 on the affair and served dinner for 178. (After the ball was over, it was brought to the

The Coronation Ball, April 23, 1937. There were seven badminton courts on which to dance.

Wine List							
SHERRY	Glass	Quart	Pint	CHAMPAGNE	Glass	Quarts	Pint
1. Harvey's Bristol Cream	.40	4.15	—	21. Mumm's Cordon Rouge 1926	—	5.00	2.65
2. William's & Humbert Dry Sack	.30	3.00	—	22. Mumm's Extra Dry	—	3.70	2.00
3. Harvey's Shooting	.25	2.65	—	23. Pol Roger Dry Special	—	4.85	2.50
4. Gonzales Byass Pale Full Rich	.15	1.65	—	24. Nathaniel Johnstons 1923	—	3.00	1.75
5. CLUB SPECIAL	.15	1.65	—	VERMOUTH			
PORT				25. French Noilly Prat	.25	2.85	—
6. Feuerheerd Commendador	.35	3.35	—	26. Italian Martini & Rossi	.25	2.20	—
7. Harvey's Old Tawny Club	.25	2.70	—	MISCELLANEOUS			
SAUTERNES				27. Asti Spumante — Martini & Rossi	—	3.35	—
8. Cruse Chateau Yquem 1925	—	4.75	—	28. Dubonnet Tonic Wine	.20	1.85	—
9. Dupont Chateau Latour Blanche	—	3.35	1.85	29. Gilbey's Brand Madeira	.25	2.50	—
10. Schroder & Schyler Barsac	—	1.65	.80	30. Chianti Ruffino	—	1.35	—
				31. Veuve Amiot Coteau d'anjou	—	1.55	—
WHITE BURGUNDY (still)				32. Chateaux Gai Champagne white	—	1.85	—
11. Schroder & Schyler Chablis Superior	—	2.05	.85	BEER ALE & STOUT			Pints
12. Hartmann Chablis	—	1.55	.80	Bass' Pale Ale			.40
				Canada Bud Lager			.15
RHINE WINE & MOSELLE				Copland's Tonic Stout			.15
14. Saarbach Sparkling Moselle	—	3.70	2.00	Dawes Black Horse Ale			.15
15. Deutz Liebfraumilch 1929	—	2.40	—	Dawes Black Horse Porter			.15
16. Saarbach Nierstein 1929	—	1.85	—	Dawes Kingsbeer Special			.15
				Dominion Special Stock Ale			.20
CLARET				Dow's I. P. Cap Ale			.15
17. Hannapier Chateau Margaux 1925	—	2.45	1.35	Frontenac Special Lager			.15
18. Barton & Guestier St. Julien	—	1.35	.75	Guinness Stout			.40
				Labatt's Crystal Lager			.15
STILL BURGUNDY				Labatt's Extra Stock Ale			.20
19. Bouchard Beaune 1924	—	2.20	1.20	Labatt's India Pale Ale			.15
				O'Keefe's Old Vienna Lager			.15
SPARKLING BURGUNDY				CIGARS			Each
20. Bouchard Sparkling Red	—	3.85	2.00	House of Lords			.15
				El Rey del Mundo, Demi Tasse			.15
				El Rey del Mundo, Perfecto			.35

attention of the organizers that, in future, care must be taken to see that members did not remove the decorations.) Mike Duggan, then vice-president, said, "Everybody you knew was there in gala dress. I saw a fine-looking friend in a grey morning coat. 'Gordie,' I said, 'where did you get that?' 'From Malabar's,' he said. I asked, 'Who did it belong to?' 'Perkins Bull,' he said." (Bull was a well-known, somewhat notorious Toronto man of considerable girth.)

At the end of the thirties, a new subject came up. The ladies, so anxious to have their locker rooms improved, finally received attention, and costs were estimated. When the figures came out — $11,000 for locker room renovations — the response came back — if that much money was to be spent the ladies would prefer to have a bowling alley instead! (There were bowling alleys at the Granite, Carlton, Victoria, and Boulevard clubs). It was an idea that had much support, and a study was done. Excavation under the badminton courts, with stairs down, lockers, and four bowling alleys, would cost around $16,000. The least expensive facility that could be built would be a new structure "on the south-west corner behind the squash courts and extending westward on ground level."

The subject was given such serious consideration because there had been a recent surge of transfers from playing to non-playing membership. It was 1939, and the club was fifteen years old. The membership stood at 1,063, of which 472 were either non-playing, non-resident, or junior. After twenty requests for non-playing status were tabled at one board meeting, a limit was put on that cate-

The uniform for assistants in the pro shop will be a maroon blazer and white flannels.
Board Minutes, May 18, 1937

"Mrs. Howard Douglas put me up for membership and I was over there playing tennis a great deal [Barbara was club tennis champion four times.] Things were very simple there. It was just like home. Once there was a tournament in which a Canadian team played the Americans in squash. The top players would come up. They had a party at the B&R for the players that were in town and Marney Lace (Grant) and I went. We weren't attached then and they wanted some unattached girls to entertain the out-of-town players."
Barbara Lace

> "When there was a party in the old lounge and dining room everyone had a great time. The B&R was the meeting place. Some members had such a good time that they would get up on the stair railings and, trying to keep their balance, would take a walk. They had bets on their success. When Courtney and I were young marrieds and had a baby-sitter, the B&R was the place we most wanted to go. The chef, whose name was Davies, came from the Royal Canadian Yacht Club (RCYC) when it closed. The meals were simple but good and then there was the big New Year's Day lunch, well attended since it was free."
>
> *Barbara Proctor*

gory — no more than 200. Whether the problem was a lack of certain sports facilities, such as a bowling alley, a desire for more elaborate social facilities, or the fact that the original members, after ten years, were less interested in racquet sports, was hard to pin down, but it prompted investigation into areas that would bring non-playing members back. A bowling alley was only one idea. Another was a golf driving alley in the north squash court.

A questionnaire was sent out asking members, and particularly non-playing members, if they would be in favour of four bowling alleys to cost $16,000, or in the enlargement of the ladies' locker room, with construction on two floors including a locker and lounge area, for $11,000. Further, if the bowling alleys were put in, would non-playing members commit to becoming playing members again for at least three years, paying $30 per year for bowling. The matter was hotly debated, but in the end it was acknowledged that times were hard and perhaps not ripe for these moves. One member noted, to applause. "I remember the struggles of the nineties of our parents. I remember every crash, every depression since then and not excepting the period of 1914 to 1918. I want to say that I think there are more people today (1938) who are worried and harried than there have been in any period of my life; there is less security, less sense of peace… I am against it." Howard Douglas said, "Ladies, we are going to have a war. We should not spend money on bowling alleys." The bowling alleys were defeated, and a more modest sum of $3,000 was devoted to maids' changing rooms. A new floor would be laid in the badminton hall, done in British Columbia fir at a cost of $3,305. Caution was being exercised in all other expenses.

The "conflagration on the horizon" was on everyone's mind. Soon there was an exodus of male and female club members to volunteer for military service.

The ladies have requested employing a man to park cars at busy times.
Board Minutes, February 17, 1938

The War Years

"Members serving in His Majesty's Forces may upon application made by or on behalf of such members be placed upon a list designated 'Members on Active Service.' Members on this list shall not be liable for any fees, and upon their return shall be placed upon the regular lists."
Board Minutes, April 1941

"Membership numbers on Active service — 203 ordinary members and 15 junior members."
Board Minutes, October 1943

"Wives of members on active service may be offered special membership (if they are not members) with no entrance fee, and an annual fee of $15 for non-playing, $30 for playing, and they will be allowed to continue as such as long as their husbands are on active service."
Board Minutes, March 1941

"A mother of two members on active service will be accorded the same status as a wife of members on active service."
Board Minutes, January 1942

"Members who served the Red Cross overseas should have the same privileges as other service people."
Board Minutes, April 1946

"They asked you to bring your children to the club during the war. They flooded the rinks over the tennis courts and served cocoa. Children were welcome in the clubhouse."
Barbara Proctor

The club was welcoming war guests, purchasing War Loan Bonds, cancelling the balance of entrance fees for some of those in the services and supporting families of servicemen in every way possible.

With many members in the services, and with national, provincial, and district championships suspended, sports activities at the club, as in all clubs, were minimized. Many of those who had represented the club in badminton tournaments or had been major contenders in club events — Bill Pinkerton, Tim Lownsbrough, Bill Scandrett, Alan Eaton and others, were in the services.

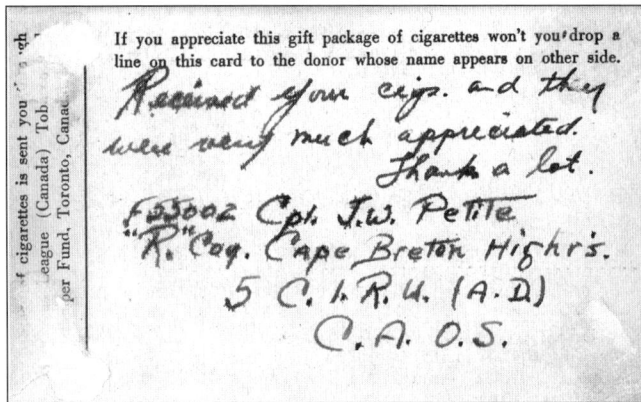

One of many thank-you post cards received by the club for packages of cigarettes sent overseas.

As a result, junior play increased. Tim Gray, Gordon Cook, and David Russell gave the juniors their full attention. The junior section was active after school hours with Bishop Strachan School, Havergal College, and Branksome Hall girls much in evidence, giving David Russell, who arranged games and was the self-appointed club cupid, a busy job of matchmaking. He introduced two new juniors, Pam McPherson and Bev Westcott, who needed no further encouragement from the pro shop. A junior round robin was arranged starting in 1943 with supper provided at no cost. A junior committee was formed with a chairman for boys and one for girls. There was one period of free coaching for juniors per week, and free coaching in December and January for the boy and girl who headed their respective ladders. Esmé Coke and Dorothy Boone gave their time and talents to these clinics. Young players joined in the many inter-club tournaments available, and the B&R was a frequent host. Senior play increased as well, with frequent outings by Bill Seagram, Fred Torrance, Fred Gundy and Jack Crean.

The absence of a great many members on active service was a matter of pride to the club, but also a matter that had to be dealt with financially. Even with all possible economies taken, the financial picture was in decline. Suspension of fees to servicemen represented an annual loss of $5,000. Two measures were introduced. A small assessment was levied — $10 per playing member, $5 per non-playing member. Members on active service, life members and juniors would pay no assessment.

The second economy brought greatly enhanced privileges with it. The Toronto Hunt Club approached the

War memorial.

home from November to April. In this way, since neither club was open for the full year, staff could move from one club to the other. Any loss or gain would be shared. Golf privileges, with no green fee, would be extended to all B&R members other than junior or non-playing. The B&R's assistant pro, David Russell, would be transferred to the Hunt for the summer season to arrange matches and use his talents in other areas. The system was endorsed by the directors and recommended at special meetings of the membership of both clubs. This was a temporary war measure only. It worked well for two years with substantial savings in staff salaries.

By 1944 a policy had been adopted that returning servicemen and women receive six months free from annual dues, and outstanding entrance fees were reduced according to the length of time in the services. A junior at the time of

B&R for a joint association, with the privileges of each club to be extended to the other's members. The Hunt Club's facilities would be available to B&R members from May 1 to October 31, and when the Hunt Club closed for the winter, their members could make the B&R their

> Resolved that an Archivist of the Club be appointed from time to time whose duties shall be to record in narrative or other convenient form, the outstanding and interesting events in the Club's history and in its activities, financial, sporting, social and otherwise, and further that the Secretary shall, from time to time, keep the Archivist informed of all matters which the Board desires to have recorded.
>
> *Murray Garden was appointed.*
> *Board Minutes, 1945*

> There is a probable shortage of tennis balls, so members are requested to buy only three per week.
> *Board Minutes, April 7, 1942*

> The House Committee report included reference to instructions from the Wartime Prices and Trade Board to collect ration coupons from staff.
> *Board Minutes, January 28 1943*

enlistment would, at war's end, be allowed to remain a junior for a period equivalent to the term of junior membership unexpired at the time of enlistment. When the war finally ended, it was suggested that returned servicemen be exempt from fees for a two-year period. At a special meeting, one returned serviceman spoke regarding these concessions, indicating that he felt the B&R had done more than most clubs in this area and that "It was time that the Members who had been on Active service should carry their weight and that such was already overdue."

On November 9, 1945, Colonel George Blackstock, the club's founder, was asked to give the Armistice Day address to the Ontario Civil Service War Veterans' Association, an honour for this twice-decorated veteran. He spoke with feeling of the problems confronting servicemen. At the conclu-

The George G. Blackstock Memorial trophy for Men's Singles Badminton Championship.

Portrait of Colonel George Gooderham Blackstock.

sion of his speech, he took his seat and slumped over, unconscious. He was rushed to hospital but never regained consciousness. He had died of a massive heart attack. One of the first to reach the hospital was Premier George Drew, for whom Blackstock was serving as deputy premier. Drew said, "Colonel Blackstock's death is a very great loss to me personally. I have lost a close friend and the province has lost a valuable public servant." And the B&R had lost its founder.

A memorial was discussed, and it was decided that a copy of the original portrait of Colonel Blackstock by Richard Jack, RA, then in the possession of Mrs. Blackstock, be commissioned. It would be hung over the front hall fireplace. Subscriptions would be taken for a George G. Blackstock Memorial Trophy for the Club Men's Singles Badminton Championship.

Post-War — Time to Re-evaluate

"The Christmas dance was on Christmas day. The first one post-war was absolutely incredible. [It brought out a record 810 members.] You had your Christmas dinner and then you went on to the B&R, and at midnight you had scrambled eggs and sausages. When everyone was home from the war the club was just jammed. You could hardly move in the place. Dancing was in the dining room and the room off it. They were sitting all over the stairs — everywhere. But then the liquor laws came in and you could not serve liquor on Christmas Day."

  Bev Westcott

"All my friends that I met socially belonged to the B&R — Mildred Brock, Esmé Coke, Rayne Macdonnell. Rayne was one of my dearest friends. We were playing doubles on the front court one day and Rayne told me that she was having trouble with her leg, so she would like me to take the short shots. When a short one came over the net I went for it and got it. It was a tough shot and I thought she would say, 'Well done,' but what she said, after seeing me from the back, was, 'Your hair is too long.'"

  Hope Salmond

"The cost of a drink minus the labour results in an eight cent profit. The cost of a dinner minus labour and material results in a thirty-six cent loss. Theoretically then a member having dinner must have four and a half drinks before the meal in order that the club break even on his dinner. I do not go on record as recommending that all members must consume four and a half drinks before they are allowed to partake of a meal. Of course these are averages. Some of our members do more than their share without even bothering to get some of it back by having a meal."

  Ramsey Fraser,
  chairman of the finance committee,
  Annual Meeting, 1948

"It seemed as if the B&R had become a men's club. The men had the best of it and they were the bosses. That was the way it was. No complaints. In the lounge all the chesterfields looked as if elephants had been sitting on them."

  Hope Salmond

"This was a playing club, but when members didn't want to or couldn't play they became tea members. Then the tea membership got large. In 1948 this club was faced with quite a problem. There were no facilities for older members. This problem split the club.... We had $110,000 in bonds. There was no waiting list. We had members who didn't want to change the atmosphere of the club, which had existed since 1924. We could slowly die eating into the $110,000 or disband and divide the money up or change the character of the club into a family club so that we would have facilities for the whole range of members from juniors right up."

Jack Crean

At war's end there were arrivals and departures, challenging changes and mundane matters. In the latter category was one thought Paul Flemming left for the incoming board. He recommended that "efforts be made to improve the language in the men's locker room."

There were significant staff changes. Coming closely together as they did, they seemed momentous. Tim Gray resigned in 1945. He had been club professional at the B&R for exactly twenty years and had made a significant contribution to the club. He was succeeded by Charlie Cutts, who came in 1947 from the Hamilton Thistle Club, at forty-seven an able and experienced teacher of the club's three racquet sports. That fall the Toronto and District badminton tournaments were held at the B&R and Charlie Cutts played in an exhibition game with the Carlton pro, his nephew, Stan Cutts, against Jack Purcell and Dick Birch. Ernie Howard recalls Charlie. "He was a fairly good size but he could get around the court well and he had a wonderful eye. He had a great habit in the winter. He had his long winter underwear on, also a vest, shirt, and coat. When he came into the club getting ready for a game, he could take the whole thing off in one piece and hang it on a hook. When he was finished he could wiggle right into it again."

No sooner had Tim Gray left than there was another change. Commander T.J. Jackson was appointed club secretary. After Roy Buchanan had assumed this challenging job at the club's opening, with Arthur Brown as his assistant, there had been Joe Lee, Major Kirby of the Indian Army, and Trevor Manning, a temporary appointment. Mr. Jackson, always referred to as **Mr.** Jackson, stayed for twenty years with one brief interlude. After his first year in the job he decided to go west and try the motel business. A current employee, Morris Squibb, was appointed to the post, a situation not to his liking, and understandably so. Squibb seemed to have a catch-all job. He was club superintendent, but during the war he was put in charge of preparing and serving light meals as well, when the steward (known simply as Hitchcock of Rosedale) returned to Rosedale in the summer. When Hitchcock resigned in 1943 Squibb was made steward full time and when Mr. Jackson left for the west to try running a motel, club secretary was added to his list of duties. Thankfully, Squibb was able to convince Mr. Jackson to come back to his job. One addition to the staff was the position of hall porter, with a desk at the foot of the stairs, equipped with a phone and guest book.

Absolutely dedicated to minute efficiencies, Mr. Jackson studied every chit signed. Bob Grant recalls that he would greet you at the door in the morning and, if you had dined at the club the previous night, would know exactly what you had eaten. He would inquire, "How was the roast beef, Mr. Grant. And the fish was all right?" Unfortunately his excessive attention to detail could ruffle feathers. Bob recalls one night when he and Marney were hosting a small party in the dining room. Bill Finlayson, then president, was there as well. Mr. Jackson came into the dining room and, bowing to all the guests, inquired if their dinner was satisfactory. This was too much for the maitre d', who considered the dining room to be his domain. He came into the room, walked over to the president's table and said, "I resign. Right now. And the chef will be leaving with me. Right now." Finlayson rose from his chair, went to the Grant table, and with supreme delegation of authority said, "Look after it Bob, will you?" Immediate diplomacy was required — a quick visit with Mr. Jackson to pacify him and equal efforts with the maitre d' and chef. The meal reached a satisfactory conclusion, and Mr. Jackson checked the chits the next day.

Joanne Morton, the club's secretary, whose charm, sense of humour, and efficiency were prime assets for the club's office from 1962 to 1998, recalls Mr. Jackson and his close attention to numbers. "He was very proper, in a pinstripe suit. When you were adding up columns of figures he would come and stand behind you and add them up at the same time over your shoulder. He was very good with the staff, but I think the members were frightened of him.

"We played doubles badminton for twenty years on Saturday mornings and as one would pass away or get sidelined another one would come in from the same age bracket. And then back in the locker room it carried on. We played in a regular league on Saturdays with the Granite Club, York Club and Carlton Club. We played inter-club matches. You knew about eighty or ninety percent of the members — George Cook, Peter Hanley, Jack Taylor, Bill Scandrett, Tim Lownsbrough, Bev Geale. I had the great privilege of playing doubles for a few years with Dorothy Walton of the Carlton Club who was a world champion.... Squibb was superintendent of the building before he became manager. If a pipe burst he could fix it with Band-Aids."

Dudley Reburn

Joanne Morton when she started in the B&R office in 1962.

> "When I was a relatively new member of the B&R Rayne [Macdonnell] came up to me and said, 'How old did you say you were?' I answered, 'I didn't say. Why did you want to know?' And she said, 'Well, if you were about twenty-one I would say you have your future ahead of you, but if you're older than that you are on your way out.' I said, 'That's the best reason I know for my not telling you.'"
>
> *Ruby Fisher*

Mr. Jackson ran things like the navy. Desk One did all the chits. Desk Two did the banking. Desk Three did the typing and minutes and oversaw the other two. So you moved up. I started at Desk One and moved to Desk Two and then Desk Three."

In the late 1940s and into the 1950s a new group of young badminton players was making news — literally. In the *Globe and Mail* the heading "Westcott Takes Badminton Title" (the 1949 Niagara Falls Country Club, New York, annual invitation badminton tournament) appeared to announce Bev Westcott's men's singles victory over rival Don Smythe of Toronto's Boulevard Club. Westcott's victory came after "three hard-fought sets" and was the first of many such headlines from that time through the 1960s. That 1949 match was followed by Westcott and Smythe partnering to win the Toronto and District doubles. In February 1951, the headline "Shuttle Player 14 Years Westcott Finally Wins Ontario Singles Crown" described the match in which "the slim 25-year-old star downed Boulevard's defending champ, Don Smythe, in an exciting final." In 1953, the headline "Westcott Trims Smythe in T&D Shuttle Upset" announced another victory over Smythe, then considered number-two player in North America. In 1955 Bev and Budd Porter were finalists in the Canadian doubles championships. Bev and Bill Purcell won the Canadian Doubles Championship in 1956. That same year Bev was a finalist in the Canadian men's singles. He won the Ontario title again in 1957, the New England Championships in 1957

> "The club had a good group of gentlemen on the board. We were very cautious about spending money. In those days you wouldn't go in the Maple Room unless you were a senior member."
>
> *Bill Parker, a member since 1928, who played tennis into his nineties*

Beverley B. Westcott
Badminton

Canadian Men's
Doubles
1956

Member Canadian
Thomas Cup Team
1955, 1958, 1961

Harry E. "Budd" Porter
Badminton

Canadian Men's
Doubles
1952, 1953, 1957,
1958

Canadian Mixed
Doubles
1952

Member Canadian
Thomas Cup Team
1952, 1955

Bev Westcott being congratulated on an Ontario singles badminton victory, by Jack Taylor, earlier Canadian champion.

Budd Porter, with a string of victories behind him.

and 1958 and was a three-time member of the Thomas Cup team, the six-man Canadian team in the international match with the United States. He added the Alberta and Manitoba titles to his list of victories. The papers described his playing as "stylish" and "smooth-stroking."

In the early 1950s Budd Porter joined the B&R with a record of victories behind him and many more to come — the first Junior Ontario Singles championship and major victories in doubles. Partnered with Don Smythe, he won the Canadian men's doubles championship in 1952 and 1953 and in 1957 and 1958. He won the mixed doubles in 1952 with Edith Marshall. He and Don Smythe reached the finals of the All England Badminton Championships. Budd represented Canada on the Thomas Cup team in 1952 and 1955.

And the young women were making their mark — Daphne Walker (First), Ann Greey (Richmond), and Esther Jackson (Eastmure) with Toronto and District victories, for Daph in Ladies' Singles, for Ann and Esther in ladies' doubles. Daph had won the Canadian Junior Singles in 1951. The *Globe and Mail* noted that in the Toronto and District tournament in 1954, "Veteran Joan Hennessey, Carlton, lost her first semi-final game in the ladies' singles to young Daphne Walker, B&R, and had to fight all the way to regain control of the match and run it out by scores of 11–8, 12–10. In the ladies' doubles semi-final Daphne Walker and Ann Greey, B&R, pulled the only upset of the night by defeating the second-seeds." Then Daph won the Granite Club twenty-first annual invitational badminton tournament defeating Canadian champion Joan Hennessey

Daphne Walker First, Canadian Junior Ladies Singles Badminton Champion, 1951.

Daphne Walker
Badminton

Canadian Junior Ladies Singles 1951

Ann Greey Richmond.

Esther Jackson Eastmure.

A new design is being planned for the front door to prevent cars from being backed into it.
Board Minutes, June 20, 1950

"Our little group would rush over to the B&R after school and sit in our lounge learning how to smoke. We would order cokes with six or eight maraschino cherries. Not one of us ever played a sport."
Billy Wilder

and leaving "little doubt of her superiority." In 1955 she was the University of Toronto's woman athlete of the year. Her marriage in 1955 meant a move to Concord, Massachusetts. She continued her dedication to sports and became a nationally ranked badminton player.

There were significant changes and major decisions in 1946. That year it was determined that $10,000 would be spent to lay Har-Tru tennis courts. This decision came after the board had communicated with the American experts at Forest Hills and received word that of twenty-two surfaces known to them, Har-Tru was the best. The Courts Committee announced that the new courts would open in the summer of that year. "Additional fees for Ordinary Members will be $7.50 and for Juniors $3.00." The decision to go to Har-Tru had huge significance for the future, as it marked the real impact of tennis at the B&R. Tennis had started as the third sport and has become the first in terms of use.

Until 1949, the club was open only from October to April. In 1949, it would be open twelve months of the year. This change necessitated a discussion: what type of dining room services would the members require in the summer months? Application was made to the Liquor Board for a license to include spirits as well as beer and wine. Two bars would be put in place, one in the men's locker room and one upstairs in place of what was a private dining room. A new class of membership, intermediate, was introduced for ages eighteen to twenty-one. Membership classes were: life, ordinary, special, non-playing, intermediate, junior, and non-resident.

Behind the scenes, however, there were financial issues to be addressed. During the war years the club had operated at a loss. The deficit for 1942 had been more than $11,000. At one board meeting the beleaguered treasurer, H.H. Lawson, described the club's financial history in graphic terms as having moved through four phases, from the initial "Constructive Building-Up," through "Coasting" to "Mild Deterioration," to the present state of "Accelerated Deterioration." The total membership was less than a thousand, and a surprisingly small proportion of

Left to right, Hope Salmond, Rayne Macdonnell, Margaret Withers, Barbara Lace in the 1940s.

the club's members were using the sports facilities. At war's end measures were necessary to increase revenue and decrease expenses. The club's first membership committee was put in place. (Until this time the board screened each application and voted on acceptance or rejection.) The membership chairman would have the authority to select his own committee, which would be a sub-committee of the board. Members of the committee would examine applications prior to board meetings. This was to expedite the processing of applications with a view to increasing membership without going on a membership drive. Revenue was needed! The official non-playing category, which hadn't been used since 1937, was reintroduced — entrance fee $100, annual fee $30. Soon forty percent of the members were in this category.

It was proposed that there be a dinner to welcome new members — stag only, with "entertainment," a tradition that began in Mr. Jackson's time, carried on for a while under Mr. Longmore, and then petered out, to be replaced

---

"My sister and I came to play in the Canadian Tennis Open. We had no lessons. She bought a book and absorbed it all. We had to take the boat to Vancouver and then spend days on a sooty train. We arrived in Toronto and were located at the Imperial Palace on University Ave. We couldn't wait for Sunday. We wanted to play all day long to get the trip out of our system. But when we went to the club there was a sign "No Tennis On Sunday." In Victoria we all played on Sunday and had tea and had a great time. That weekend my sister won the ladies' singles. She and I won the ladies' doubles. She and John Proctor went in the mixed and won and Ken and I got engaged. Then we went home. Two years later my sister and I represented Canada in the U.S. Open."

Hope Salmond

"I joined in 1949. Mac King was a well-known figure around Toronto. He took a great personal interest in Ernie Howard and followed his career closely. I remember Jack Taylor, so fast on his feet, and Bob Springer. John Proctor used to love to come around the club. He came regularly on weekends. His cronies would come in and the repartee would be turned on. Doug Hamilton was a member of the board and good at racquet games with a quick mind and quick with the repartee as well. When he and John Proctor were there the jousting took off. Doug and Tom Boynton were a doubles squash team. Tom Boynton was a really great racquets player, and his sons, as well. I remember Jack May, president in 1958. He was a good hockey player and had the record of scoring three goals in the shortest time ever at Maple Leaf Gardens. And Wally Halder and George Mara distinguished themselves by being picked out to play hockey in Switzerland in the Olympics. I think that this kind of good sporting people attract like-minded people to the club."

Jock Maynard

"You had such a happy time in our era of playing. If you lost and you knew you were beaten you didn't care. The club was small and you wanted it to stay the way it was for the rest of everybody's lives. You knew everybody in the club. Hope and I played together for fourteen years without a harsh word between us. In those days we would play with the same tennis balls all summer."

Ruby Fisher

Would members please refrain from using the parking lot unless they are actually visiting the club.

*Twenty-fifth Annual Meeting Report
(and so on for the next fifty years)*

> "Wednesday lunch has been going for years. They just drifted in. There might be ten or sixteen at a big long table. I remember sitting there when U.S. President Kennedy was killed. We were all there in the back room. The men's area was booming on Saturdays. There would be at least three bridge games going on and then as well there were the men who had been playing, had a shower and stayed for a drink."
> *Dudley Reburn*

> "Pug Hunter's trademark was to have one hand in her pocket. She was so adept that she could drop the bird with the right hand that held the racquet and rally."
> *Ann Richmond*

by an all-member cocktail reception. But traditions die hard and memories of those stag nights are fresh and clear today. Chink Fleming, a club tradition himself, was a mastermind in these affairs, as he has been in every aspect of club life. He can still regale his listeners with tales of Tessie the Tassle-Twirler or Twinkle Star.

Other economy measures were introduced: sending out letters indicating that "posting" might be invoked for non-payment of fees; closing the skating rink (which was made by flooding the tennis courts), closing Saturday night dances at 1:00 a.m. unless a member offered to pay to extend the time; reductions in staff and food; discontinuing of English magazines (many complaints resulted); increasing the price of soft drinks and increasing the squash fee from fifteen to twenty-five cents. And then that dreaded word, "assessment" was introduced. The proposal was to assess members $15. After an adverse reaction, this was reduced to $10.

Members were still disturbed and requested a special meeting — request declined! And, finally, the practice of having dinner served to the board at the club's expense was discontinued temporarily.

It was time to look to the future. The club was at a turning point — to stand pat or to change? The Reconstruction Committee, appointed in 1945, had a mandate to recommend alterations, additions and improvements, and to retain an architect if necessary. It reported to the annual meeting the following year with certain goals. They were: better locker room accommodations, especially for the ladies; kitchen, dining and changing space for staff; locker rooms for junior boys and girls so they would not have to use the public rooms of the club; enlarged dining room and lounges; better cloakrooms, and a proper place for the pro and the hall porter.

Reconstruction plans were put on hold, however, for three to five years, as the club was "in a period of transition," meaning that operating losses were still a problem. Losses were as much as $14,000 in 1947. But plans were drawn up, the goal to improve facilities for members. Bowling alleys under the badminton courts were mentioned again. They were found to be a costly item, at almost $60,000 for four alleys with spectator seating under the parking area and a lounge under the hall. Strong beams and steel columns would be needed under the parking lot. While not approved, the idea had persistent support and would not be totally discarded.

> One member was suspended for a year for misdemeanors. His father would have taken it very badly had he known. So every day after work he visited a friend with a flat at Yonge and St. Clair, had a sleep, showered, combed his wet hair, and went home. Every day the result was the same. His dad always said, "How was your game today." For a year the answer was always, "Not bad."

The president, R.F. Wilson, reported financial concerns to the 1948 annual meeting. "Our major financial problem is due to the fact that only a small proportion of the membership at large uses the Club facilities and this problem will last indefinitely in our opinion as long as we have to keep an organization set up for over 1,000 members when less than half that number use the Club. Do you realize that out of our membership of 1,200 members there are only about 600 active house accounts and on this active list there are many members who are only in the Club once or twice a month."

Alterations to the club house were finally approved at a meeting that lasted until midnight. There would be a ladies' locker room and powder room on the site of the two badminton courts at the east end of the Badminton Hall, a new lounge on the second floor above this, the existing men's locker room to be split to incorporate new office space, a cocktail lounge in the former office space. The upper lounge would no longer be needed, so most of its space would be added to the dining room.

The proposed structural changes, to cost $90,000, were highly controversial. On the one hand, they were seen as totally changing the nature of the club from its original purpose, strictly a playing club with some simple dining accommodations, to a more social club. On the other hand they were seen as providing facilities to accommodate the increasing number of non-playing members by providing space for them to enjoy social events in the new lounge and bar. Ramsey Fraser explained how costs would be met. The Club would take in 40 to 50 new members, use reserves, take out a mortgage or loan of $20,000, and sell $44,000 in bonds. In explaining the concept of family memberships, Fraser noted that husband and wife together would have their membership at a reduced rate with children free. But he said, "Everyone must come up for membership individually before becoming part of a family membership. This way we avoid taking in a family as a group and then finding out

> "There was a famous competition. The two parties had to have a combined age of over ninety years. In the finals Dr. Fraser and I were playing against Jim White and Fred Torrance. Fred was pretty good, so I said, 'Let's give 'em to White and keep it away from Freddy.' I think there was one thousand dollar bet on the game. There were two hundred people watching. All my friends bet on me. We won."
> *Mike Duggan*

> "Jackson would buttonhole a member as he or she came into the club and say, 'Your account is overdue.' The names that were posted were put on a board covered by a blank white sheet. It was like a red flag to a bull. Everyone lifted the sheet to look."
> *Ernie Howard*

> "Back in the forties dominoes was very popular. There were always about three tables of dominoes that would get going after work — Gordon Wills, Fred Gundy, Peter Gooderham, Bill Seagram, Deacon Jarvis. There were A, B, and C tables. Then backgammon started. Sandy Watt, one of the real characters in the club, was a backgammon player."
> *Bev Westcott*

"We were very active with inter-club matches in postwar badminton. You would get people to go to the Carlton Club, the Granite Club, which was along the street, the Boulevard Club (it seemed like going to Hamilton to go there) and the Strathgowan Club (not too popular as the showers were no good.) On Saturday afternoons there was usually a team of seven to nine players and there was a certain amount of socializing — a match, then another — then sandwiches. I used to play badminton regularly with Esmé Coke, Jack Crean, Freddy Torrance, Alan Eaton, Bill Scandrett, Bev Geale, George Cook, Tim Lownsbrough. They all joined in the thirties. There was a club called The York Club that folded some time in the thirties and that's when we got a lot of these members. I played with Bill Pinkerton after the war. He was ranked eighth in Canada. Doug Hamilton and Fred Gundy were good badminton and squash players. We would fill seven badminton courts Monday through Friday.

"Esmé Coke was very slim. She teamed up first with Dorothy Boone and then in the fifties with Dorothy Walton. She probably had the finest cut drop shot of any player I ever played with. She would always bring out new birds and Freddy Torrance would bring one new bird and two or three older birds. Then he would tip all the birds over so it wouldn't be known he only brought one new one. This went on week after week, and we knew what he was doing."

Bev Westcott

"If the girls got a date Wednesday they wouldn't be at the B&R Thursday or Friday. You couldn't get a team to go to the Boulevard Club on a Thursday or Friday because the girls were all washing their hair. David Russell paired a lot of our friends off. The old pro shop was very small, where the phone booth is now, with a window that looked over court three. He would be hanging out the window encouraging the kids."

Pam Westcott

"John Proctor and some of his friends came to the Members' Lounge on Saturdays to watch the afternoon football game. John would settle in with his big cigar. One day a little kid came in. He sat down to watch, and then he got up and started changing the channels to find something he liked. It didn't last too long. John said, 'Young man, I think you had better find something else to do.'"
Ernie Howard

"For most of one winter there was a group of workmen sitting eating their lunch against the wall [during some construction at the badminton courts] while badminton was being played. They had never seen badminton and when the championships were played they were spellbound. We had a captive audience — clapping, cheers. Never had there been an audience who found us so gripping."
Ann Richmond

"My first recollection of the B&R was that my mother liked badminton and took me over there. We had played quite a bit of badminton in the back yard and in Temagami, and so now I could be taken to the B&R. Mom said, 'Here comes Mrs. Coke and she is a champion beyond belief. Don't forget to curtsey.' We went up and Mom said, 'I'd like you to meet my daughter, Ann.' I curtseyed. Mrs. Coke was thin, with knee socks, and riveting brown eyes. She said, 'Are you a badminton player?' I said I loved the game. She asked me to show her how I held the racquet. She passed me hers. I reached out and shook hands with it. She looked down and said, 'Well, you may make a badminton player.'"
Ann Richmond

"We all went right over to the B&R after school, from BSS, UCC, Havergal. We were all there looking for a date for the weekend. Mrs. Olive Gooderham and Mrs. Jane Garden made a point of being there at exactly that time to check up on us. If you put your feet on the table they would tell you to take them off. As soon as we saw them coming we all sat up straight because they would report anything back to our parents."
Cherith (Coke) Howard

"Inter-club play was very active in the fifties and sixties. Every Saturday afternoon the B&R squash team would play another club. You'd pick a team of eight, nine, ten players. They were graded one to ten. The two 'ones' played and so on."
Jock Maynard

that young junior is a proper stinker."

And then there was that issue that would not go away. The ladies were being heard from again. In February 1944 they made another tentative approach to the board on the subject of having representation through a lady member. The reply came back that there was nothing further to add to the previous letter to the committee on this subject, that their presence on the board would make it unattractive to men. Issue put to bed again. Undeterred as ever, the head of the ladies' committee expressed the feelings of the women that communications with the board were inadequate, if not nonexistent, and that their committee should be supplied with a copy of board minutes and be kept informed by the club secretary of proceedings of board meetings. The reply came back that board minutes were strictly confidential and therefore not available to the ladies' committee. There would, however, be an effort made by the chairmen of committees to inform ladies of matters that they felt would concern them. The ladies requested that prices be shown on the à la carte luncheon menu. Request turned down. They requested that a list of committee members be posted. The board decided against the suggestion. Negative feedback to all these decisions was palpable.

There was, however, one step forward. A request to have sandwiches served in the ladies' locker room had previously been denied, but now that their locker room was to be newly enhanced, with a powder room, it was decided to leave the decision to the ladies' committee. There was one proviso, however. Never on Saturday! Suffice it to say that the other issues were not dead.

In 1949 the club marked its twenty-fifth anniversary. The membership numbered 1,502. Celebratory events were held in 1950 — a gala anniversary dance in costume, with a grand march and prizes for the best portrayal of a well-known 1925 character, the most authentic 1925 costume, the funniest 1925 costume. It was billed as the best B&R party ever. If so, that was quite a boast.

Notice of dance.

Revellers in costume.

Left to right: Barbara Bowen and "Boy" Bowen, Betty and John Kennedy, Bill and Betty Parker, Babe and Boyd Somerville, Jeff Boone at the back.

Left to right: Bill and Barbara Heintzman, Yvonne and John Poupore, Patsy and John Hanley, Howard Heintzman, and Pauline Coulson in 1924 costume at the twenty-fifth anniversary dance.

The Golden Age of Squash

"The squash players would have liked to have all their matches here on our court. It was an expensive court at the time [1957]. The wooden walls made it so good because you can get truer shots. Wooden courts today are too expensive. We were the premier squash club in the city then. Until the seventies we were the leading squash club in Canada —the Montreal Badminton and Squash Club (MBSC) came close. Our two clubs had the two best club pros in Derek and Doug McLaggan. In the very first Pro-Am squash tournament at the B&R in the early 1950s every player was met at the airport. Derek had a great feel for that sort of thing. He would say 'That's what you have to do. Let's get a bed for everybody and put them in members' homes.' Every single player said that was a great idea. That's how the B&R got the reputation for running the best squash tournaments."

Ian Stewart

"In the men's locker room there were a few full-sized lockers that would hold a suit. After I won the Ontario Doubles in squash Mr. Jackson called me and said I could now have one of the large lockers."

"Ernie Howard beat me in the club squash finals twelve consecutive times, then I beat him once. He came back, beat me the next year, and then retired."

John Foy

"Otto was the Hall Porter. He took care of bookings and arranged games. He was a true Prussian, a bit of a character with a heavy German accent. I had a game at five-thirty and for some reason it got cancelled and I was never told. I rushed to the subway and then to the club where I found I wasn't playing. I said to Otto, 'Why didn't you call me?' 'Oh,' he said, 'You come here every day so what's the difference?'"

Ernie Howard

"After careful study, it was decided to provide an additional parking area on the tennis courts, which, if successful, could be added to as required [parking would be on the boards which covered the courts in winter]. While the cost was considerable, it was felt that it would help the patronage of the club. I personally feel some regret in doing away with such a perennial topic at the annual meetings and one which could always be counted on to enliven our evening. I have no doubt, however, that the ingenuity of the members will bring out something probably worse to take its place."

Paul Greey

"I believe we now have one of the finest clubs in Canada on an extremely low-fee basis, a club in which all can take justifiable pride."

Ramsey Fraser

Ramsey Fraser's recollections of squash at the B&R begin with the opening of the club:

"When my parents became charter members at the birth of the B&R in the autumn of 1924, I was thrown into the package as one of the earliest junior members. From that lovely vantage point I witnessed the construction and opening of the 'first and only' doubles court in Ontario. Located on the east wall of the club together with two singles courts, it was assembled by transforming the old machine shops of the Toronto and York Radial System."

These courts were a huge drawing card in 1924, bringing in members from The Toronto Racquet Club and The University Club. As well, the Club had a squash pro, Tim Gray, from 1925. The B&R produced some outstanding squash players. Jack McCausland, with his Montreal partner, H.D. Lancaster, won the inaugural Canadian Open Doubles Squash title in 1934, and Jack won nine B&R singles squash championships. Christie Clark, Geoff Beatty and C.C. Radcliffe were leading players, as was Jack Chipman, also a Canadian champion.

But in 1936 the original doubles court was closed for lack of use. "The one and only doubles court in Ontario," wrote Fraser, "alas became redundant due to lack of interest and play and the area became known as the Lower Bar and subsequently the Members' Lounge." In those early days, noted Peter Watson in a recent speech entitled *Squash Walls of Fame*, "Members had to look to Montreal or the Eastern U.S. — New York, Boston and Philadelphia- for a really decent game." Land was purchased "just to the south of the badminton shed," and by the end of the year three new singles squash courts and a gallery had been opened there. The new courts were hailed as the finest in the country. They were in use for the Canadian Squash Championships in 1936 when the B&R welcomed players and put on a dinner and dance for eighty and a buffet lunch for fifty.

The Canadian Squash Championships were held on the new courts again in 1940 and 1948, when Doug Hamilton reached the semifinals and "Pete" Peterson won the Consolation. Money would be set aside, $25 each for three squash players, to attend the Lapham Cup match in

> Squash racquets, a descendent of the centuries-old game of rackets, was first played at Harrow, England, in 1850. Boys who were waiting to play on the rackets courts began hitting side-wall/front-wall shots to each other, as a way of passing the time. Rackets was originally played outdoors, but as squash courts developed they moved indoors to courts built as additions to some of England's larger homes, then to British boarding (public) schools and to army and navy garrisons. With this move a smaller racquet and an India rubber ball were found to be suitable. Singles squash courts were smaller than the old rackets courts (which were similar in size to the court now used for doubles squash), the smaller court being appropriate to the pace of the rubber ball. The name of the new game came from the squashy sound made by the ball, a softer version of the much harder rackets ball, when it hit the walls of the court.
>
> Like badminton, squash was brought to Canada by British military officers stationed here in the late 1800s. The first Canadian squash championships were held in 1912. A year later, three clubs, The Montreal Racket Club (founded in 1810), The Toronto Racquet Club, and The Hamilton Squash Racquets Club, banded together to form the Canadian Squash Racquets Association. The game initially had little chance of catching on in a broad way in Canada, however, since, unlike badminton, which could be played in the ubiquitous church hall, the only squash courts were in private clubs or private schools. By the end of World War Two Trinity College School, in Port Hope, had the most active squash program, followed by Upper Canada College and Ridley College. Courts were built at the University of Toronto's Hart House in the 1920s and at McGill shortly thereafter. As a result squash became known as a "gentleman's game."
>
> Squash came a long way from those beginnings as a sport for the privileged. Its tremendous growth was marked by popular development programs for young players all across the country, with levels of play giving opportunities for different abilities. Squash became the fastest growing indoor sport in Canada. Part of the history of the game is the use of goggles, now mandatory, after successive eye injuries.

David C. Higginbotham
Squash

Canadian Junior
Men's Singles
1948

Philip A. Greey
Squash

Canadian Junior
Men's Singles
1954

Hartford. This great traditional annual competition, friendly but highly competitive, between squash teams consisting of fifteen Canadians and fifteen Americans, was started in 1922 by Henry Lapham, who gave a trophy for what were, until then, informal matches. Players one to five were top-ranked in their country, six to fifteen chosen on the basis of skill and services to the game as well as personal sociability.

By the end of World War Two squash was becoming more popular at the B&R, much of the interest generated by young men who had played the game at private schools. The Little Big Four Squash Championship was held at the club many times from 1945 on. Trinity College School (TCS) sent out a stream of champions. Eight of the fifteen members of the Lapham Cup team in 1938 were TCS men. David

Higginbotham and Phil Greey, two young TCS men, each won the Canadian Junior Singles. And then, in 1953, the accomplishments of TCS grad Ernie Howard became a source of pride for Canadians and a cause for great celebration at the B&R when he captured both the U.S. National Singles Championship and the Canadian Singles Championship in the same year.

On February 23, 1953 young Ernie Howard walked into the B&R to a rousing welcome, back from his victory in the United States National Squash Championships in Buffalo bearing the title that was a cause for unbridled celebration. He had just done what had never been done by a Canadian before, following his win in the Canadian National Singles Championship in Ottawa with the U.S. title. It was a feat described with relish by W. Stewart Brauns Jr., president of the United States Squash Racquets Association, and U.S. representative to the International Squash Racquets Federation. Brauns said, "For me, remembering the tournament is akin to remembering my most recent glass of 1955 Chateau Lafite-Rothschild."

"When [Ernie] Howard and [Cal] MacCracken went on court [to play the finals] the atmosphere was electric with tension…. Contrary to some of his contemporaries, Howard did not ring changes with his game plan. He was first, last, and always a proponent of what was taught as holy scripture by the famous Yale coach John Skillman; volley, volley, volley….to facilitate his volleying skill he used a

Ernie Howard, centre, being congratulated by Mac King, left, club president, and Charlie Cutts, right, club pro, after his victory in the U.S. Singles Squash Championship.

light racquet with the balance toward the handle. He would dart around the court like a drop of mercury on a sheet of glass….Ernie started with a rush to take the first game 15-9. From a 10-10 tie in the second game Cal won it 15-11. The Canadian came back to garner the third game 15-12. There then occurred one of the game's great historic cameos. Seated in the front row was the brilliant and controversial gentleman Edwin H. (Ned) Bigelow, a self-made Wall Street millionaire. Arguably he was the greatest innovative supporter of the game. For example, he went on to

"Squash doubles is still growing with more categories — the early years plus 55, 60, 65, 70, 75 — all the categories. In the old hardball game of squash they quit about 40. Now with the softball game in the U.S. they have an over 85."
Ian Stewart

Ernest Howard
Squash

U.S. Men's Singles
1953

Canadian
Men's Singles
1953

> "Back in the early fifties on Friday night the B&R was the great gathering place — a whole gang watched the Friday night fights. After several drinks Doug Hamilton would issue a general challenge, 'I could win at squash with a tennis racquet.' And every time Burke Smith would rise to the bait. Hamilton always beat him."
>
> *Bev Westcott*

found the U.S. Open and the National Junior Singles Championships. Loyal to his beloved New York City, being a son of Brooklyn Heights [MacCracken was from New Jersey], he stood, turned around to face the gallery and threw down the gauntlet by shouting, 'Where is that Canadian money?' The rush of Canadians wishing to place bets nearly pushed Ned backward into the court. Jim Traviss, Canadian S.R.A. president, happily acted as bookkeeper. For a while it looked as though Ned would be vindicated as MacCracken took the fourth game 15–10. In the fifth game the score seesawed to another 10–10 tie when Howard moved out to a 14–11 lead. At that point Ernie inexplicably hit two straight shots into the tin. However, MacCracken, on the next point, returned the favor and the match was over amid ear shattering Canadian cheering."

It was, according to the *Telegram* in Toronto, "the first U.S. National title of any consequence won by a Canadian individual since the early thirties when Sandy Sommerville won the U.S. amateur golf championship. This was the first time in the 42 years the U.S. Nationals have been held that a Canadian has advanced beyond the second round." Ernie Howard was the first member of the club to win a U.S. or Canadian title; the first Canadian to win the U.S. title; the first Canadian to hold both titles; the first Canadian in 18 years to win a U.S. amateur championship of any kind; the first squash player to take the title out of the United States since 1924 and the second player to do so in the 46 years the title had been in existence. A testimonial dinner was held at the club on March ninth, and Ernie Howard was made an honorary life member.

Squash aficionado Ian Stewart calls the twenty years from 1945 to 1965 the "golden years of squash at the B&R." He said, "It was certainly the leading squash club in Ontario, if not in the entire country, measured by the number of champions produced, number of players and number of major championships hosted. During these twenty years, along with his major 1953 victories, Ernie Howard won thirteen club championships, as well as numerous Ontario and

Left to right: Peter Hanley, Bill Minton, Doug Hamilton, John Foy, Mel Jones, having won the Ontario Team Squash Challenge Cup in 1952.

Toronto and District championships. He was unquestionably the outstanding player in Canada during the 1950s and early 1960s. In that same period of time [1945 to 1965] David Higginbotham, Phil Greey, John Ireton, and David Bassett won national junior championships and although we never produced a doubles championship team, our players were nearly always semifinalists or finalists." In 1953 Tom Boynton won the Canadian Open Doubles Championship with a partner from Montreal, as had Jack McCausland before him. "In the Ontario team championships and the Toronto and District leagues," said Stewart, " we were more often than not the champions, and such famous players as Peter Hildick-Smith (British amateur champion in 1952), Jeff Short, Mel Jones, Doug Hamilton, Harold Peterson, Jim McMurrich, Peter Gooderham, Peter Hanley, Tom Boynton, John Foy, Bill Minton, Bill Hatch, and Fred Gundy are mentioned in numerous press dispatches and directors' letters."

Enthusiasm for squash was booming, and B&R members were winning titles in every area from A and B city leagues in Toronto and District matches in Ontario and in Canadian levels, with strength among the juniors that ensured squash titles for the future. "This enthusiasm for the game, not just at the B&R, but across Canada," says Ian Stewart, "had much to do with the accomplishments of Ernie Howard."

In 1953 the inaugural Canadian Pro-Am Singles Tournament was hosted by the B&R. There were six pros and ten amateurs, and a great final match took place between Ernie Howard and Doug McLaggan, pro at the

> "What are the characteristics of the B&R? The racquets games are related. If someone is good at one he will be good at another. Youngsters may begin with badminton and then move to tennis or squash and then, later on, there are doubles tennis and squash. You have a concentration on racquet games in this club. Then there is good family participation. If you like racquet sports your kids probably will, too. And long-term membership is a real characteristic of this club. There are many three-generation families here and some four-generation. And, of course, location has always been in our favour."
>
> *Jock Maynard*

> "Tom Boynton was an exceptional squash player. The peak of his years were the war years. I was sent up from TCS and I played him in the first round of the Ontario championships in 1946. I was old enough to know that he wasn't working very hard while I was running around the court. He allowed me to get eight or nine points. We were standing around after the match and Mr. Boynton was right next to me. Someone asked him, 'How did you do?' He said, 'I was very lucky.' I said 'Oh, Mr. Boynton, please!'"
>
> *Ernie Howard*

Tom D. Boynton
Squash

Canadian Men's Doubles
1953

Robert P. Bedard
Tennis

Member Canadian
Davis Cup Team
1953, 1955, 1956,
1957, 1958, 1959,
1960, 1961, 1967

Canadian Open
Men's Singles
1955, 1957, 1958

Canadian Open
Men's Doubles
1955, 1957, 1959

Canadian Closed
Men's Doubles
1970

Member Canadian
Pan American
Games Team –
Silver Medal
1959

Member Canadian
Stevens Cup Team
1985

Inducted into the
Tennis Hall of Fame
1992

Montreal Badminton and Squash Club. Ian Stewart notes that this "was the forerunner of the tournament that later became the Canadian Open Singles and now is known as the North American Open." The B&R's Pro-Am tournament and the Canadian Open were later amalgamated because players often had to choose between tournaments. Most opted for the Canadians because of the ranking. John Bassett, who had given the Pro-Am trophy and $500 a year for the arrangements, was in support of the change. The first merged tournament was held at the B&R. The Pro-Am tournament was highly praised in squash circles in Canada and the United States, and introduced Hashim Khan, a relatively small, stocky, very talented squash player from Pakistan, and his whole extended family of squash players, to fascinated spectators. "I was secretary of the pro association then," says Derek, "and I called in a few debts to get them."

With interest in squash at a high at the club, the subject of a doubles squash court came up, the first since the original doubles court had been taken out in 1936. A new doubles court was built. It cost $54,000, and was reinforced to accommodate another doubles squash court on top in future years. It was opened in 1957. Ernie Howard said. "The most outstanding and widely travelled players in the world made the statement that the new doubles court was the finest they had ever seen." The official opening took place in February and included a piper, a

Doubles squash court in action in the 1960s. Left to right Pep Hunter, Doug Musgrave, Kemmis Martin, St. Clair Balfour.

ribbon-cutting and exhibition play with prominent guest players invited from the Granite Club, the MBSC, Montreal Amateur Athletic Association (MAAA). From the B&R, players were Ernie Howard, John Foy, Tom Boynton and the club's pro, Derek Bocquet.

There were new names and new titles. In Ian Stewart's *History of Squash at the B&R* he notes that "in the 1960s John Foy and Johnny Bassett won half a dozen Ontario championships between them and Foy and Peter Stewart produced an Ontario Doubles Championship. Terry Corcoran and John Bassett won three club singles championships and John Foy added one to the win he had in the previous era. John Foy and Peter Stewart dominated club doubles play during most of the 1960s." At the Veterans' level the names Whelpton, Boynton, Hamilton, Whitaker, Hatch, Minton, Mills, and Jennings came up on the winner's board. Tony Wells won the Manitoba Singles Championship as an out-of-town member and the B&R Veterans' championship back in Toronto. When the Canadian Lapham Cup team defeated the United States in 1960, seven of the fifteen members were B&R men — John Bassett Sr (captain), David Bassett, John Foy, Lew Gunn, Bill Hatch, Julien Hutchinson and Tony Wells. Don Leggat, who was with the Hamilton Thistle Club then, but later joined the B&R, was also on the team. Leggat won the Canadian Open Singles in 1961. Over the years he won twenty-five more national singles and doubles titles. And there were impressive wins from new names in the 1970s: Victor Harding, John Boynton, Peter Hatcher, Robin Logie and Howie Rober.

Then in 1958 there was a first at the B&R — the Ladies' Singles Squash Club Championships with eleven entrants. The finalists were Elizabeth (Betty) Parker, who had started playing squash at the MBSC in 1937 and joined the B&R in 1950, and Mary Taylor. A trophy was given for women's squash singles that year and named in their honour. Mary Taylor won the first two championships, and after a hiatus, Betty Parker won two in a row, followed by Barbara Heintzman, Winifred Welch, Judy Traviss, Karen White and, in 1970, Nancy Henderson and Susan McElhinney (Behan).

Judy Traviss made her mark in squash in a dramatic way. She took up the game at age 18, having already had significant success in tennis. Judy was ranked ninth in Canadian tennis in 1964, and seventh in 1965 and 1967

Judy Traviss, pioneer in women's squash.

Don E. Leggat
Squash

Canadian Men's
Singles
1961

Canadian Men's
Veterans Doubles (40+)
1970, 1972, 1975, 1976

Canadian Men's
Doubles (50+)
1981, 1983, 1986

Canadian Men's
Veterans Singles
Hardball (40+)
1970, 1973, 1974

Canadian Men's
Singles Hardball(55+)
1984, 1987

U.S. Men's
Veterans Doubles (40+)
1971, 1974, 1975, 1976

U.S. Men's Senior
Doubles (50+)
1981, 1983, 1984, 1985, 1986

Canadian Men's
Singles Hardball (60+)
1993

World Masters
Men's Doubles (50+)
1986

World Men's Doubles (60+)
1994

and, still young herself, took a great interest in junior tennis development. She won four Quebec Singles Squash Championships from 1965 to 1969. One Quebec opponent called her flat shots to the sidewalls "deadly." Judy was a semifinalist in the U.S. Women's Singles Squash Championship and won the Massachusetts State A Singles Championship. She was semi-finalist for the Howe Cup Tournament in Philadelphia. With her father's financial support and her dedicated drive, she put together a team of women to play for the U.S. Team championships, the Howe Cup. They surprised everyone by winning the B division and putting Canada on the women's squash map. A Canadian Women's Championship came next, with Judy using her contacts to get top U.S. women to participate. Judy Korthals and Nancy Henderson from the B&R were key in these arrangements. Judy Traviss was also the driving force behind the formation of the Ontario Ladies' Squash Racquets Association. (In the first provincial championship in 1972, the hard ball was used in the A championships and the soft ball in the B.) This remarkable young woman, when not on the courts, was president of the Canadian Daily Stock Quotation Service.

After Judy's untimely death from cancer at thirty-two, she was honoured by the establishment of the Judy Traviss North American Open Singles tournament. And "fittingly," notes Peter Watson, "our own Sue Behan won the Judy Traviss North American Open Singles title in 1978. Sue has unquestionably been the strongest player at the B&R over the past twenty-five years." As a teenager Sue was a badminton player, but when she failed to be chosen for an inter-club tournament with the Granite Club she decided to try squash. Soon she was in tournaments. As well as her victory in the Judy Traviss in 1978 Sue played in the North American Open Singles, held at the B&R, and was on the Canadian women's squash team on its trip to England.

The switch to the soft ball had an enormous influence on women's squash. Many women took up the game

Barbara Heintzman and Judy Traviss, at the club singles tennis championships finals in 1971 with Charlie Dalton.

> "This anecdote concerns the annual Parent and Child Badminton Tournament. From the time Squirrel (Cyril) Andrewes got Toronto mad about badminton, Ma ["Elf" Fergusson, an original member] was a keen player. She was a very sporting person generally…. However by her mid-fifties she had given up badminton…. Three days before this Parent and Child event, which was bigger cheese than it is now, Ma came into the club and was greeted by the long-time stalwart who manned the desk…. He said, 'Mrs. Fergusson, I have entered your name with your son in the tournament and I have a bet with Elsie, the matron of the ladies' locker room.' Ma said, 'I have retired, you know, but if you have made a bet — well, a bet is a bet….' So I was recruited and Ma rummaged around to assemble a badminton costume…. and a somewhat warped racquet. After all, she was just going to put in an appearance.
>
> At eight-thirty we were slated to play a thirty-something mother and her eight-year-old son…. So we played and won. [Then] the fellow at the desk said 'Mrs. Fergusson I've called a few of your friends and told them that you are playing and they didn't believe me and are coming to cheer. (Dorothy Boone, Olive Gooderham, and "Pick" Harris and others.) By the time we were on the court for the second round there was a gallery. By the third round at noon it was an event! We reached the finals by mid-afternoon. Ma said, 'Look Blair…. I've had it. It is you against them. I am holding up my racquet and if the bird hits it okay, but I'm not running for anything.' We lost. [When the cry went out for the presentation of the runner-up's prize] Ma said 'Oh, thanks, but I have no time for that, I have to go bowling.'"
>
> *Blair Fergusson*

at that time. One was Trish McElhinney, Susan Behan's mother. Her granddaughters, the third generation of squash players, are learning at the club today. For real enthusiasm, however, it is hard to surpass Maggie Corcoran who, wearing an especially designed maternity outfit, played until the day before her first child was born. The outfit was made by Joan Stewart, and was passed on to other women squash players.

The story of squash at the B&R has to include two people who contributed greatly to squash at the national and international levels. James Traviss was president of the Canadian Squash Racquets Association from 1952 to 1954. He was also the first non-American to gain the President's Cup, sponsored by the United States Squash Racquets Association, and awarded to the "person who

Blair Fergusson, Katy Mahoney, and Blair's daughter, Kira. Continuing the generations.

A squash team of British Ladies visited the B&R and trounced the B&R men. This was noted in the ladies' committee minutes of January 10, 1963, but not in the club's board minutes.

has made a substantial contribution to the game of squash racquets."

Ian Stewart received the same prestigious award in the 1980s. He was president of the Canadian Squash Racquets Association from 1964 to 1966. He was elected an honorary member of the U.S. Professional Squash Racquets Association in 1964, the first Canadian so honoured. He served on the World Squash Association, a body started in 1967 in England. Coincidentally on a business trip to England at the very time of that first meeting, he attended as Ontario president even though neither Americans nor Canadians had been invited. The United States and Canada were made associate members, then became full members in 1971. Ian was a board member, and served a four-year term as president. Ian Stewart and Ernie Howard have travelled with the Jesters, a group formed in England in 1926 in which experienced players assist racquet sports in schools and universities. There are branches around the world, including one in Ontario. B&R men have contributed as presidents of the Canadian Squash Racquets Association — Jack McCausland, Douglas Philpott, Ian Stewart. Ernie Howard served three terms as vice-president.

Much credit for the popularity of squash at the B&R

Ian Stewart, a great contributor to squash associations.

In the gallery. Jimmy Traviss with Jim Prendergast and Barney Lawrence on the left and Roland Michener and Ian Stewart on the right.

Four friends, all past presidents. Left to right: Bill Hatch, Ramsey Fraser, John Foy, Peter Stewart.

must go to those first professionals who contributed so much — Tim Gray who was appointed squash pro in 1925, Charlie Cutts, who took over from Tim Gray; and Derek Bocquet, a ranking professional in England who was British professional champion in tennis singles and doubles in 1951. He was a finalist in the Canadian Professional Squash championships in 1953.

A fitting climax to those golden years of squash came in February, 1970. It was the story of an indefatigable pair, Peter Stewart and John Foy, and, of course, Peter's bride, Joan Stewart. "When Joan and I were married," says Peter, "I asked her where she wanted to go on a honeymoon. She said we weren't going anywhere. 'You and John are going to win the Ontario Squash Doubles.' We had our wedding reception at the B&R and we went to the Inn on the Park. By that time Joan had a temperature of 104. She was sick for five days. John and I went to the tournament. I have never seen Foy so psyched up! We managed to get to the finals on Sunday morning playing Don Leggat and Bill Bewley. And we won. Afterwards I said to John, 'I feel funny.' I bought a bottle of champagne to celebrate and then, like my bride, was sick for five days."

The story hit the press.

"HONEYMOON DELAYED FOR A SQUASH TITLE

Peter Stewart was married on Thursday but the honeymoon hasn't begun yet. Instead he spent the weekend playing squash with John Foy, capturing the Ontario Doubles Championships at the Badminton and Racquet Club. Their victories came after a 15-5, 13-15, 17-14 18-14 battle against third-seeded Don Leggat of the Hamilton Thistle Club and Bill Bewley from the Toronto Cricket, Skating and Curling Club. Bewley, a former Alouette football player, gave full credit to the finesse and steadiness of the champions."

Derek Bocquet — Tennis, Squash, and his Juniors

"Once I was in a board meeting at Southam's. Murph called to get me for a game and my secretary told him that I couldn't be reached as I was in the middle of the meeting. 'Well,' said Murph, 'then get him out!'"

St. Clair Balfour

"I told them that they might think I was nasty, but they could never get along without me. I was always informed that this club would close if I left."

Murphy

"It is very difficult to produce national champions today. It takes work, work, work. People have too many other interests. I don't care if we ever have another national champion as long as players are having fun."

Derek Bocquet

Tennis is the oldest racquet game. It dates back to the thirteenth century, by which time there were twelve tennis courts in Paris. When it became popular with the kings and nobles in France it was played in castle courtyards, where any architectural irregularity became part of the game. By 1600 it was the national sport in France. An English visitor was reported to have said, "There be more tennis players in France than ale drinkers in England." There were 1,800 courts in Paris and 2,500 scattered throughout France in spaces that included walls and local hazards. It eventually became standardized into "court," "Royal" or "real" tennis. Court tennis is still played in England and in four or five U.S. cities, where wealthy Americans have built their own courts. The "tambour," the "dedans" and the "penthouse" above the court are permanent fixtures, which the ball can hit and from which it can carom off. The net is high at the sides and low in the centre. The word "love," meaning zero, came from the French "l'oeuf," the egg having the shape of zero. The game became popular in England when Henry VIII took it up in 1520 and brought it to Hampton Court where the oldest "real" tennis court is still in use.

Major Wingfield of Great Britain devised the first rules of tennis in 1873 and patented the game under the name of Sphairistike. This, happily, was changed to Lawn Tennis and made its way to Bermuda in 1874, then to the U.S. The Toronto Lawn Tennis Club was founded in 1876. The first Wimbledon tournament was held in 1877, men only. The following year the first tournament was held in Canada at The Montreal Cricket Club. In 1900 the Davis Cup was inaugurated. Canada entered a team thirteen years later. B&R members Gil Nunns and Bruce Harrison spearheaded the formation of the International Lawn Tennis Club of Canada. The magazine, Racquet Canada, published in 1971, was the inspiration of Ernie Whelpton.

"The best time in my life was when I worked here," says Derek Bocquet, and that, in the light of his previous careers in England, is quite a statement. Derek came from England in 1951, first to The Hamilton Thistle Club, then to the B&R in 1953. With him came a set of credentials probably little known to B&R members. Starting in Prep School, where he was the only boy in the school's history to play for his school in five different sports, Derek continued at Cheltenham College, on first teams in cricket, tennis, squash, and field hockey. He won championships in Junior Outdoor and Indoor Tennis (Wimbledon) and was ranked the number-one junior tennis player in England. At Sandhurst he played first team tennis, squash, golf and field hockey and got colours for four sports in the same year.

In 1938 Derek was told by the British Tennis Association and the British Golf Association that he must make up his mind which sport he wanted to play for England. He couldn't play both, as the training programs clashed. He chose tennis, packing in his "serious" golf at age 18 with a two handicap. He played tennis for England at Wimbledon before the war, saw service in the war years, was awarded a Military Cross at Dunkirk and returned to play tennis and squash for his country. Derek turned pro in tennis and squash in 1947, trained to teach lawn tennis, squash, Royal tennis, fives and rackets. He won the British Pro championships in tennis and squash

Derek Bocquet, pro from 1953 to 1984.

three years later. Derek was offered the position of head pro at Wimbledon, but decided instead to move to Canada. "The pay was so ridiculous I turned it down. Once I came to Canada I gave up playing tournaments seriously as I wanted to concentrate on teaching. But," he adds, "I am totally inept at skiing, skating, piano playing, riding, bridge, poker, scrabble, and mah-jong."

At the B&R Derek entered into tennis and squash with gusto. He also started what was perhaps his greatest contribution to the club — his junior tennis clinic. His

Derek R. Bocquet
Tennis

British Junior Men's
Indoor Singles
1936

British Junior Men's
Indoor Doubles
1936

British Men's
Professional Singles
1951

British Men's
Professional Doubles
1951

juniors were promising, and he brought their promise to fruition. "I divided them into groups — the most promising twelve and then the next. It was exciting working with them. Any pro who does not say, 'My main object is children,' should not be a pro at a private club."

In 1954 Derek requested permission to hold a tennis clinic for twelve talented junior players from the T&D during July and August, four of whom would be B&R members. An extra pro would be made available to free his time for this special undertaking.

Then, in September, Derek led a tennis course for exceptional juniors. Sponsored by the Ontario Lawn Tennis Association, it was highly successful. Three star B&R juniors were Peter Barnard, John Bassett and Mary Nunns. The finalists and winners of the Ontario Junior championships were all from Derek's course. In the Canadians his sixteen-year-old players made it to the semifinals and were only defeated when confronted with the seventeen- and eighteen-year-olds. The following year Peter Barnard and John Bassett Jr. won the Canadian Junior Open, the first Canadian team ever to do so. They also won the Ontario Junior Open and Peter Barnard was runner-up in the Ontario Junior Men's Singles.

On their way to the Ontario title, their prowess caught the attention of the local media:

John F. Bassett
Tennis

Member Canadian
Davis Cup Team
1959

Canadian Open
Junior Men's
Doubles
1955

Canadian Closed
Junior Men's
Doubles
1955

Derek with the 1950s tennis clinic, assisted by John Bassett Jr.

"A lanky young pair from the Toronto area recorded Canadian junior tennis history….at the Rideau Club yesterday. Johnny Bassett of Toronto and Peter Barnard of Oakville teamed to win the open junior men's doubles final from the Montreal and top-seeded pair of Geoff Black and Smith Chapman in a grueling two-and-a-half-hour match. It marked the first time of an all-Canadian final and thusly was the first win by a Canadian pair in the seven-year junior history. Bassett and Barnard [are] both participants in the Bocquet-Dimmer-Mansfield-Cutts junior development clinic in Toronto."

In 1958, Derek's juniors won virtually all of the Ontario and Canadian Championships. Two of his stars, Harry Fauquier, who had won the Canadian National Junior Tennis Singles in 1960, the first time that title had come to the B&R, and John Bassett, were invited to play in Davis Cup trials — two out of ten Canadian players to be invited. Both were chosen for the team. Harry Fauquier was on the Canadian Davis Cup Team nine times between 1962 and 1973, and was captain of the team in 1972 and 1973. "Harry," says Derek, "had so much power and natural talent. Shot-wise he was the greatest." Derek's annual junior clinic for top players became the Ontario Junior Development Clinic held for three days in August. It became a preparation course for the national championships.

Harry Fauquier and Greg Halder, both Canadian champions.

The B&R and its outstanding junior program were synonymous. Brenda Nunns won four tournaments in Under Fifteen including, with her partners, the Canadian National Junior Doubles and the Ontario Junior Doubles, and she was a finalist in three others. (With David Bassett's win in the Canadians in squash, it was a clean sweep for the B&R in junior tennis and squash.) Brenda went on in 1962 to win the Toronto Telegram Junior Ladies' Singles and, in 1965, the Canadian Open Ladies Doubles. She was on a Canadian team to play against the U.S. In 1962, Nunns women won all the club tennis titles. Brenda won Ladies' Singles, with Mary as runner-up. Brenda and Ruth won

Harry E. Fauquier
Tennis

Member Canadian Davis Cup Team
 1962, 1963, 1965, 1966, 1968, 1969, 1971 Captain 1972, 1973

Canadian Open Junior Men's Doubles
 1959

Canadian Open Junior Men's Singles
 1959

Canadian Closed Junior Men's Singles
 1960

Canadian Open Men's Doubles
 1968

Canadian Senior Men's Doubles (45+)
 1987, 1989, 1991, 1992

David E. Bassett
Squash

Canadian Junior
Men's Singles
1960

Brenda Nunns
Tennis

Canadian Junior
Doubles
1962

Canadian Open
Ladies Doubles
1965

> "Harry Fauquier was in his late forties and playing for the club championship. His young opponent was wearing him down in the finals. At one point when the ball was sitting on the service line the young man ran to the net, jumped over, ran to the ball, picked it up, handed it to Harry, ran back, jumped over the net and, when he turned to receive the serve, said OK."
>
> *Bob Grant*

Bea Nunns with her four daughters, Ruth Grant, Brenda Shoemaker, Margot Northey, and Mary Gordon and their husbands during an annual family round robin.

Ladies' Doubles, with Mary and her mother, Bea Nunns, as runners-up, and Brenda won Girl's Singles. Wally Halder and partner won the Canadian Open Senior Men's Doubles in 1968. Wally was on the Gordon Cup Team and won the doubles match, the second time in twenty years Canada had won. And there was Judy Traviss, outstanding at tennis and squash, "She could play any racquet game," says Derek. "She played tennis like Navratalova did." The boom in tennis activity at the club was spurred on by the inspiring play of the club's stars in national and international play.

For two of those outstanding juniors it was all in the family. Brenda and Mary Nunns are two of the four daughters of Gilbert and Bea Nunns, and in that family tennis is a passion. Gil Nunns, who, with Bea, joined the B&R after the war, was Ontario, Quebec and Canadian Junior Men's champion in 1924 and 1925 and won five Ontario Senior titles in singles and doubles between 1929 and 1931. He was ranked number one in Canada in the 1930s, and played on seven Davis Cup teams between 1927 and 1934 and captained the squad against the United States that last year. "Playing for our country," said Gil, "with the likes of Art Ham and Walter Martin was an experience I'll never forget. We played whenever we could, but the demands of our careers made it difficult sometimes. Our off-court conditioning usually involved only running — we didn't have time for anything else. When we travelled in Canada or the United States we were given a daily allowance of $6,

The Nunns family. Three generations of tennis stars, on the occasion of the election of Bea and Gil Nunns as Members of the University of Toronto Hall of Fame. Gilbert and Bea, centre. Daughters Mary Gordon, left, and Ruth Grant. Grandaughter Gillian Grant, right.

Gil Nunns, Bob Winters, Bill Minton, Walter Martin, relaxing after their regular Saturday noon game in the 1960s.

"When I came from England no pro ever wore shorts."
Derek Bocquet

"Otto was a real character. He couldn't get his mouth around Wally Halder's name. He always called him Holly Walder."
John Foy

"We decided to open the waiting list in 1976. We opened it one day and there was a line-up along St. Clair down to Yonge Street. We got 150 to 200 applications in one day."
Ian Stewart

which went further than you'd think." Gil and Bea's daughter, Mary Nunns Gordon, described her father's style as, "So smooth and graceful. Think of Bjorn Borg. That's what he was like in his sixties. What a wonderful forehand." And that forehand was described as, "the best I have ever chased around a court" by Bill Tilden, the king of tennis before World War Two. Gil Nunns said, "My forehand was my strongest stroke. There was a little top-spin but it was largely flat." In those days, when professional tennis was unheard of and there were not millions of dollars in the picture, Gil had to give up serious competition to pursue a career. Invited to Wimbledon, he had to refuse. "If I'd gone away for six weeks, I'd have been unemployed when I got back." Often he would be working on a Saturday morning, and no matter how intense his match that day might be, would have just enough time to catch a bite and rush to the courts. Bea Symons Nunns and Gil met through tennis at the University of Toronto. Bea was number-two tennis player in Canada at the time of their marriage and won numerous provincial, regional and national tennis titles. Gil and Bea were inducted into the Sports Hall of Fame at the University of Toronto in 1989,

> "We had a succession of bartenders at the B&R. Big Lou was very attractive to the ladies. He was six foot four or five and very handsome. At the monthly dances Big Lou kept the bar open to midnight and after."
> *Bev Westcott*

> "During the summer there might be a whole group of men in the Members' Lounge whose wives were at the cottage. One was asked, 'Are you going to take any holidays this year?' 'What,' was the answer, 'and spoil my vacation?'"
> *Anonymous*

the first couple to be so honoured. Gilbert Nunns was inducted into the Canadian Tennis Hall of Fame in 1993.

In 1963, ten years after Derek became pro, he found he had new and unique company in the pro shop. Ken Finch, his assistant pro, a "county player" from England, was in place and doing well, as well as Barry Taylor, who, Derek maintains, "Could play anything. He was the best all-round athlete I have seen." But there was a new man, Murphy, on the job arranging matches. Originally in the permanent force in the army, Murph came to the B&R as a bartender. He became an integral part of B&R lore. Murph stories are legion. For instance, Joanne and Diane,

Barry Taylor, assistant to Derek Bocquet in the 1960s.

> "Derek was a wonderful pro and a gentleman with a great sense of humour. Ken Langmuir came in to lunch after his lesson and said to Derek, 'I have spent hundreds of dollars on tennis lessons and I still can't play!' Derek said, 'Do you think you should be getting a message?' Doug Musgrave and I played a lot of squash together. When we won the doubles we were put in the A division the next year. We were soundly beaten. We were put back in B, and Doug asked Derek why we were in the B league. Derek answered, "Because there is no 'C.'"
> *Bob Grant*

working in the office under Mr. Jackson's eye, were given time at three o'clock to get a soft drink from the bar. One day when Joanne set off to get the drinks she got a surprise. 'There was a little bell at the bar you could ring,' she recalls, 'and in a minute I heard this gruff voice —"What do you want?" "Two fresh lime drinks," I said. The reply came from the back. "That's too hard for me." The next thing I knew there was Murph holding a big frozen fish and waving it in the air at me as he started to chase me.'"

One day Murph broke his arm. Management, in its wisdom, decided to move him to the pro shop in charge of booking courts and arranging games, a unique and popular service. That gruff voice became known to secretaries around the city. He had a list of their phone numbers and

Murphy at the phone booking games. The name of every member's secretary was in that file.

entered the 1950s showing a healthy profit of more than $12,000, but the financial report revealed that the surplus was almost entirely due to the club's thriving bar income, this being a situation discouraged by the Liquor License Act! Land in the St. Clair and Yonge area was becoming more and more valuable, and so the club's assessment was increased. The membership barrier, which had stood at 1,400, was lifted, with a gradual increase to 1,600 approved by the board. By 1966 the total had reached 1,956 but was back down to 1,646 in 1968. A new neighbour had appeared. Fran Deck had opened his restaurant on the adjacent vacant lot. Windshield tags were introduced to keep trespassers out of the parking lot.

There was interest in another sport. The subject of a swimming pool had the endorsement of approximately 150 members. A committee of ten prepared a report. The proposed location, between the south tennis fence and the club boundary, would allow for a pool of 60 feet by 25 feet, with a patio at the east end and a high wooden fence, an attempt to keep the noise away from the tennis courts. The cost, $25,000 to $30,000, brought a halt to immediate

would brook no opposition in getting through to his man. If, when he reached his man, he got a negative answer, he would retort, 'What do you mean you can't?' Typical is one instance John de Pencier remembers well: "My secretary got a call from Murph. She rushed in to tell me Murph said it was an emergency. It was about a game of seven o'clock tennis." Bob Grant remembers the time Murph phoned him about a game of tennis. "I asked who else would be playing. 'Oh,' said Murph, 'so-and-so and so-and so and I'll get the fourth from the cemetery.'"

There were, as always, financial matters for the board to deal with. A fee increase was necessary. The club had

> The great Bruce Harrison of Seniors fame
> Can remember his score in every game
> Way back to the days of Rene Lacoste
> Except for the ones he actually lost!
> *B&R Newsletter*

Nancy E. Doherty
Tennis

Canadian Junior
Ladies Doubles
1965, 1966

Canadian Junior
Mixed Doubles
1965, 1966

Canadian Senior
Ladies Doubles (35+)
1988

Canadian Senior
Ladies Doubles (40+)
1988

Canadian Senior
Ladies Indoor
Doubles
1988

Platform Tennis

Canadian Ladies
Doubles
1981, 1982, 1983,
1985, 1987, 1988,
1989, 1991, 1992

Robert P. Bedard
Tennis

Member Canadian
Davis Cup Team
 1953, 1955, 1956,
 1957, 1958, 1959,
 1960, 1961, 1967

Canadian Open
Men's Singles
 1955, 1957, 1958

Canadian Open
Men's Doubles
 1955, 1957, 1959

Canadian Closed
Men's Doubles
 1970

Member Canadian
Pan American
Games Team –
Silver Medal
 1959

Member Canadian
Stevens Cup Team
 1985

Inducted into the Tennis Hall of Fame
 1992

1965 renovation. Ian Stewart and Bill Finlayson inspect the work. One photo before the work, showing two chimneys.

implementation, and the plan was put on the back burner, passed on, with other such contentious matters, to the new Advisory Planning Committee, a group of former presidents and directors whose role was to be a sounding board to "recommend, suggest and advise," and who would be linked to the board through the current president. They would look at capital projects for the next five years, to the mid-60s, with all the extras that came up for discussion — curling, indoor tennis, bowling, golf on the tennis courts, and that thorny question of parking — to build under the badminton courts or under the tennis courts? Their report

Early Bird Tennis

It is thirty-five years since the idea of a 7:00 a.m. tennis group hit the first eager participants, and now there are more than thirty on the roster and on the courts bright and early twice a week, Tuesday and Thursday. The originals were Pooh (Sidney) Harrison, Bridget and Ted McMurrich, Margaret (Pug) Hunter and Joe Nixon, followed soon by Jim Stuart and George Henderson. Once the bubble was erected and the group had grown, Jim Stuart organized a schedule and the Early Birds filled four courts. A mixed-age group, they are known for their skill at "power tennis," their long rallies and their stamina.

And their enthusiasm does not stop when they leave the courts. Many occasions seem to demand a party. In fact, since they play on Tuesday and Thursday, any special day that falls on a Tuesday or Thursday cries out for recognition. On Maundy Thursday the Queen gives out gold coins and the participants have English beer. On Labour Day they drink screwdrivers, on Armistice Day French 75s. On Bubble Up day they drink champagne and on Bubble Down day it is Australian champagne, of course. There has been Early Bird Ski Day and après-ski at Osler Bluffs Ski Club courtesy of Bill Barrett, an Early Bird supper party at Lil and Harry Seymour's, and an 8:00 a.m. Christmas party in the sports lounge, that featured carols with a contemporary twist. Two weddings have resulted from the convivial meetings of this group.

A toast to the raising of the bubble by some of the Early Bird tennis players who frequently fill the courts at 7:00 a.m.
Jim Stuart, Lynn McEachren, Sheila Connell, Eric Ryerson, Ann Laidlaw, Bob Reeves.

raised the questions that would lead eventually to major construction. The firm of Mathers and Haldenby was employed to make plans.

Estimates for improvements were presented in 1964: $300,000 for a larger men's locker room, a junior boys' locker room, and a junior mixed lounge, air conditioning for the lounge, bar and dining room; a room for private parties (initially the Gold Room, now the Blue Room); a changing room for male staff; second floor washrooms; an enlarged pro shop, and other improvements. An increase in fees, a bank loan and cash on hand would pay for the improvements, with the bank loan to be paid off in five years. At a

"A lady came to see me and asked for a lesson. She told me that she had never been on a court, but her husband played a lot of tennis and they were leaving for Bermuda tomorrow and she wanted to learn how to play tennis today."
Derek Bocquet

Elizabeth Graydon, Barbara Proctor, Sheila McGillivray, Mary Lash, duplicate bridge players whose memberships in the club total more than 250 years.

One Tuesday afternoon in 1967 an activity took place that causes some members to say today they belong to the Bridge and Racquet Club. Elizabeth Hunter and Willo Mills arranged for Kate Buckman to lead a few tables of bridge. (The winners of the first tournament were Willo Mills and Bea Nunns.) Today there are nearly one hundred players each Tuesday afternoon, many of whom have been B&R members for more than forty years. Early problems included drafts in the winter and too much air conditioning in the summer. Finally one convener threatened participants with instant electrocution if anyone touched the thermostat. There were chairs that ruined stockings, an unpopular cut-off time of four o'clock, too much traffic around their tables and lunches consisting of "crêpes of undetermined origin, and cardboard cookies." In spite of these setbacks there has been a thirty-four week season, Christmas bridge, Jackpot, No Zero, with lottery tickets as prizes, guest day, and a charity game once a year where each player donates to the American Contract Bridge Association for its annual charity gift. Mrs. Lyman Howe, an original B&R member and a perennial winner at the bridge table, donated a silver tray, which is a coveted prize today for the ladies' duplicate bridge. Now Nancy Sabina has succeeded Kate Buckman and Michael Davey, who taught many years with Kate, leads entertaining and informative bridge lessons several times each week. A mixed duplicate evening became a popular monthly event. Bridge, an intellectually athletic activity, is now included in All-Events Days.

general meeting in January 1965, with 150 members present, the addition was explained, questions were asked and the proposal was carried. When the construction was completed there were opening events. The remaining original members were recognized at a men's dinner (36 originals attended) and a ladies luncheon (60 of the original 81 were there). There was also a dinner and dance with souvenirs for the originals, a tie for the men and a leather jewellery box with the club crest for the women. A racquet design for the entrance was approved, three different racquets in polished aluminum, at a cost of $1,400. Change takes time to be absorbed, but gradually the Blue Room, a dining room- party room- bridge room, and site of the summer Bistro, became one of the club's most popular spots.

> "Ruby Fisher and I played Tom McCarthy and Judy Traviss. Tom is a very swashbuckling guy. We were warming up and Tom came up to Ruby and said, 'Well, Grandma, are you ready?' She turned to me and in that delightful voice said, 'Lets kill'em.' We won the toss. I had to serve to Judy and she gave a short return and Ruby hit this overhead and it went between Tom's legs about two hundred miles an hour. We beat them about 6-2, 6-1. At the end Tom came up to Ruby and said, 'I'll never call you Grandma again.'"
> *Peter Stewart*
>
> "Bruce Harrison never forgot a score or a shot. He was a very good tennis player. He was Mr. Tennis. After a game at the Queens Club we were all sitting around and then, suddenly, in a quiet moment, Bruce Harrison said, 'And then at four-all in the final set I decided to lob.' We all broke up laughing. He was a real character. He played all over during the war. He got into all the officer's tournaments and he could remember every set of those overseas matches. He lived and breathed tennis."
> *Peter Stewart*

> "There was a painting of two prostitutes. [It was purchased by Dolly Proctor and Gerald Larkin, who were appointed by the directors to buy a painting for the club]. It used to hang in the lobby but one of the members didn't think it was fitting for the club and slashed it. That made it even more interesting and now it hangs in the dining room."
> *Bob Grant*

A decorative piece for the bar, a weathervane of a running horse over a steel ball, [complete with dents where it had been fired at by a gun] was obtained by R.W. Finlayson, from his sister, Mrs. J.W. Eaton, to be returned to Mrs. Eaton if and when it is no longer needed.
Board Minutes, December 1963

The meticulous Mr. Jackson was due to retire. The date was set. His successor had been chosen. He was Lieutenant Commander Wigmore, a "paybob," or paymaster in the Navy in Halifax, and had been recommended by Mr. Jackson, as a possible successor. The board was suitably impressed, at least initially. Wigmore was to start training with Mr. Jackson but the secretary manager took ill and went into hospital. He died in June, 1966. Wigmore was not in place yet and so the versatile Morris Squibb took over for a brief period. Joanne Morton, the club's secretary, carried on office procedures between Mr. Jackson's death and the arrival of his successor. The board singled out Joanne for high praise: "Mrs. Morton's ability to understand what the B&R is all about, and her coolness under fire, are irreplaceable." Wigmore, however, was not. He took over with no training and his tenure turned out to be brief.

Morris Squibb was also due to retire. His replacement was being sought and the answer was Chief Engine Room Artificer Norman Longmore, soon to retire from the Navy. He would come to train under Mr. Squibb as a "stationary engineer." When Squibb retired Norman Longmore was appointed club manager in his place and was in charge of

Wally E. Halder
Tennis

Canadian Open Senior Men's Doubles (45+) 1968

"We could field the best tennis team and the best squash team. Even when the Toronto Lawn was so good we could still field a good team — Harry Fauquier, Johnny Bassett, Mel Jones, John Foy, Peter Stewart, Peter Barnard, Ernie Howard and Bruce Harrison — our number one team."

Derek Bocquet

Club Manager Norman Longmore 1966 to 1986, with Fred Gundy.

The officers of the Royal Yacht Britannia will be given tennis privileges at the club during the Royal visit June 29 and June 30. Officers of NATO ships will also be given privileges when visiting Toronto later in August.

Board Minutes, June 22, 1959

"Margot Nunns and I played against Bassett and Barb Bell. Bass was six foot six and he was really intimidating Margot. We were almost out of the game. Bass said, 'I wonder what the prize is?' I turned to Margot and said, 'If it kills me we are going to win this match.' Bass was hitting to Margot's backhand. We changed that and managed to beat them. When we were shaking hands I turned to Margot and said, 'I wonder what the prize is?' Bassett nearly exploded."

Peter Stewart

maintenance, personnel, bar service and the dining room. Joanne Morton, as secretary, would be in charge of office personnel and membership.

Then a question that had not been raised for some time was put to the board in 1965. It was quickly set aside on what must have seemed like a permanent hold. A letter from Barbara Proctor suggested that the lady members of the club might be better served by having three of their number be part of the twelve-member board. The reply came back that the ladies' committee should perform the job for which it had been set up! Barbara Mabee, chairman of the ladies' committee in 1968, brought up the subject again. The women thought that their chairman should automatically be a board member. As ever, the answer was notable for its originality: "No one by virtue of their position is a member of the board but is selected for their ability to fulfill certain functions such as legal, financial, or courts."

"In thinking of plans for the future, care should be taken to ensure that the club retain its distinction as a racquets club.... This club was formed on and owes its success to the fact of its being a racquets club and this should never be lost sight of. If it were, then it would lose the charm that has held us together for so many years."

*Mr. May
Annual Meeting, 1954*

Fifty Years and on to the Diamond Anniversary

Bar drinks will be reduced in size to 1¼ ounces as an economy.
    Board Minutes, January, 1976

There have been numerous complaints about the reduction in size of bar drinks.
    Board Minutes, February, 1976

The House Chairman reported that the size of bar drinks has gone back to normal.
    Board Minutes, April, 1976

"When Terry Corcoran first joined the club he was obviously very keen, certainly very aggressive and in very good shape. I was having a regular game with him and he was struggling. He said to me, 'Tell me what I am doing wrong.' I told him, with tongue in cheek, that he had to be more aggressive, that he wasn't trying hard enough. Of course he was so aggressive that he would almost die on the court before he lost a point."
    Ernie Howard

Terry Corcoran, a few well-chosen words at prize-giving with Peter Hatcher.

In 1974, on the eve of the fiftieth anniversary, plans for the celebrations were moving ahead. Two teak boards would be ordered to list the names of all the club's presidents. The four-day anniversary weekend would start Thursday with a black-tie recognition dinner, honouring original lady and gentlemen members, past presidents and those who had achieved athletic distinction. The next evening would be a gala dinner and dance for all, followed on Saturday by special racquet activities and on Sunday by a family luncheon as sumptuous as the New Year's day luncheon. An evening of reminiscence was slated for senior

Before the fiftieth anniversary dinner.
Cyril Andrewes on the right.

The fiftieth anniversary dinner in 1974. Head table guests are: Doug Bassett, Billy Wilder, Mac King, Dorothy Boone, and the president, Bill Hatch.

men, with drinks and dinner to jog their memories. This would be taped to provide meat for a history, to be called *The First Fifty*, by Arthur Bishop.

The men's dinner began with some fascinating recollections by Roy Buchanan, Graeme Watson, Mac King and John Proctor. As the evening wore on, tales emerged, such as the story of the women's showers, a problem that blew up in Mac King's presidency. The ladies had complained that the water from their showers spilled over the bottom ledge and onto the floor and that stepping out was a hazardous procedure. A delegation of five highly competent board members, having warned the women to vacate, examined the problem. When it defeated those experts they called in plumbers. None could find a solution. Then someone thought to ask Mr. Jackson. He took one look, headed for the local hardware store and bought smaller showerheads. Problem solved.

The ladies' committee held a series of lunches to honour their original members. Undoubtedly there were drinks to jog their memories, as well, but unfortunately for posterity, the confidences exchanged were not taped. One thought that survived from 1924, however, was, "This [new club] was something unique and it sounded like fun. For once the girls were not only included, they were allowed to be part of that sanctuary of sanctuaries — the club."

The B&R was in demand. The membership had topped 2,000 in the early 1970s and was hovering around 2,100 — a total the board thought should be held. Prospective members could expect at least three or four years on the waiting list (after four years an application must be dusted off and updated) and even the prospect of annual fee increases did not deter their enthusiasm. The fees were on a steady upward climb — an increase of $25 for senior members in 1970, another $25 to $190 in 1972, 15 % in 1973, another 15% in 1975 and 1977 to $341 for seniors. Entrance fees were climbing as well. By 1979 the entrance fee for a senior members was $2,500.

There was an interesting development that spoke to the aims of this family club. There were relatively few openings for new members because there was a continuous flow of young members working their way up through the membership list into intermediate, then senior categories. The waiting list was closed, a fact that caused some concern for financial gurus. The imbalance of children of members on the list, while healthy for the club's future, caused concern in the present because new senior members were the ones who would be free with their money. By 1977 the membership was at 2,352 and holding, and by the end of the decade there were 500 on the waiting list, in spite of that steady climb in entrance fees.

But the club was struggling financially, and the problem was aired at the 1976 annual meeting. At least

> "Doug Musgrave was almost entirely unflappable. Nothing really upset him and nobody could have been more understanding of the staff. Take this incident. One day, while in the locker room, he ordered a steak for lunch. George, the attendant, duly brought in an appetizing-looking T-bone steak. Unfortunately, as he was a little unsteady, the steak slipped off the plate and fell on the locker room floor. George quickly pushed it back on the plate. 'Oh, George,' pleaded Doug, 'could you bring me another one. This one looks a bit soiled.' Off goes George to the pantry, picks up a used, sopping wet towel, wipes the dirt off the steak and re-serves it to Doug, who, as always, the perfect gentlemen, thanks him profusely."
>
> *Derek Bocquet*

$25,000 a year was needed for renovation costs to be financed by increased entrance fees and annual fees. The board was given the power to raise fees by 15% "when they deem necessary." All fifty-year members had been made honorary life members in time for the fiftieth anniversary, a situation that brought honour to those involved while at the same time causing a leak in the financial reservoir.

Activity was brisk in every direction. A great compliment had come to the club in the fall of 1970, fittingly in Ernie Howard's presidency. The B&R had been asked to host the North American Squash Tournament in January

1971, a tournament that came to Canada only once every eight years. The massive organization necessary was undertaken with gusto, even with an expected deficit of $1,000 or more in the background. Club members were contributing in the world of squash. Ian Stewart was serving as chairman of the International Squash Racquets Federation. (In 1978 he received two honours — the Queen's Silver Jubilee Medal for his "contribution to squash throughout the world" and the Ontario Special Achievement Award for efforts on behalf of squash in Ontario.)

There was a continuing increase in tennis activity after the installation of lights. Meanwhile the three-court tennis bubble (or "babble," as it was not so fondly called — you couldn't hear a call from the other side of the court because of the echo) was causing problems with dust and there were whistling sounds coming from the doors. All this disquiet came to a head one day when an emergency exit was pried open and the whole structure collapsed. New locks were ordered, and an inter-room phone installed to allay the fears of some members who thought they might be locked in and trapped if the bubble came down.

Club tournament entries were up, and Murph, otherwise known as "Head Bookie," was hard at work co-ordinating more than 200 matches. Peter Gordon, chairman of the courts committee in 1975, lauded him for planning the daily timetable for the squash, tennis, and badminton courts and somehow managing "to co-ordinate successfully the playoffs for 50 various club championships of all sports combined. Some of these events, such as the handicap matches in squash and tennis, have as many as 150 entries. They are surely the biggest club tournaments in North America." By 1978 that record had been eclipsed in the club's handicap tennis — 180 entries for men and 80 for women.

There were some outstanding victories beyond the local scene. Young Greg Halder won the Junior Davis Cup

> "One problem we had those many years ago was the introduction of strange 'local rules' by some members. What would you make of a statement by your opponent, 'Let's rally for serve.' This would be a very long and tedious exercise, especially as one was not allowed to try to hit a winner, but even more astounding was a commonly accepted statement from one's opponent when they came up to serve, 'First one in counts.' Anyone who let Bill Wilson get away with that one was in serious trouble. Coming up to serve, he would let fly with a series of thunderbolts, which, with luck, you could dodge out of the way of as they whizzed by your ear and crashed into the netting on the fly. Eventually he would get one in the appropriate court, but as likely as not you never saw it as you were cowering behind the roller. Bill would announce, with a perfectly straight face, '15-love.' Apparently the three consecutive double faults didn't count. Oh what a wonderful group they all were. Some of them are sorely missed."
>
> *Derek Bocquet*

Greg R. Halder
Tennis

Member Canadian
Davis Cup Team
1977, 1979

Canadian Closed
Men's Doubles
1980

Canadian Closed
Men's Singles
1980

Tennis Tournament and was semifinalist in the Canadian Closed Junior Singles, third in Canada in his age group. In 1973 he won the Ontario Junior, then played at Wimbledon in 1977 and 1978, in the Italian Open and in the French Open. He stood 130 in the world in singles tennis, 120 in doubles, was runner-up in Canadian Singles, and was a member of the Davis Cup Team. Harry Fauquier won the Western Ontario Singles and the Nova Scotia Singles.

In squash the cub was on the international winning scene again. Victor Harding was ranked number three and then number two in Canada. He won the Toronto A, was runner-up in the Canadian National Softball Squash Championship and was on the Canadian four-man team competing in the world championships in England. Then came his victory with partner Peter Hall of Hamilton in the U.S. Open Doubles, the first time Canadians had won this event. That same year, 1977, Vic reached the finals of the U.S. Amateur Singles and followed that with a 1978 win in the Canadian Doubles and Ontario Singles. These victories would be capped by wins in the U.S., Canadian, and Ontario Doubles championships in 1981. When Ernie Whelpton scored a further victory in the U.S. by defeating Lyman Smith in the first Seniors Over 70 Squash Tournament in Albany, New York, the quip at the club was, "It is reliably reported that the Canadian

Greg Halder with Peter Stewart.

Tom McCarthy and Victor Harding in the 1970s.

Susan C. Behan
Squash

Judy Traviss
North American
Open Singles
1978

Department of External Affairs is actively working to restore diplomatic relations."

Squash was increasingly popular across the province. In 1972 there were 3,000 squash players in Ontario. By 1975 there were 30,000. From the B&R the team of John Foy and Peter Stewart were finalists in the Canadian Veterans' Doubles and won the Ontario Veterans' Doubles. The Judy Traviss North American Open Ladies' Singles was held at the club in February 1978 and won by the B&R's Susan McElhinney-Behan, who had emerged as an outstanding player. She represented Canada in the British Ladies' Open in 1978. An exhibition match between Susan and Sandy Morgan

Sue Behan and Ann Thompson at a prize-giving dinner, 1981.

stimulated great interest. Pam Davidson won the Ontario Ladies' Singles and in 1981 became a member of the Canadian Ladies' squash team. Ann Thompson was also chosen for the Canadian Ladies' Squash Team and would tour Britain and play in the Ladies' World Open. During this time the club regularly hosted Canadian and international competitions and continued with round robins and the city league. A husband and wife squash tournament was held for the first time at the club and was a great success.

Badminton activity having decreased in the late 1960s, an indoor tennis mat was laid on the courts on

Well-known squash supporters at the North American Squash Tournament in 1971. Colin O'Shea, Ernie Howard, Bill Hatch, Barney Lawrence, Ron Gunn.

alternate days to make use of the space and to provide facilities for the overbooked tennis courts. But with the arrival of Barry Taylor, who encouraged both junior and senior play, the caliber and amount of badminton increased again. (Barry was considered the logical successor to Derek but left the club in 1978 for a career in another field.) The Wansbrough girls, Susan, Jane, and Ruth, could take on a challenge from anyone and distinguished themselves in T&D leagues, and in Ontario and invitation junior tournaments. In 1972 Susan Wansbrough won the Under 14 Ontario Girl's Singles and in 1973 she won all club events for under 14. At 15 she won the Ontario Singles and Junior Doubles and was on the winning Ontario team at the Nationals.

Jane and Ruth Wansbrough in a finals against Ruth Grant and Nancy Doherty. The referee is Budd Porter.

Nancy Henderson, helping juniors in the 1970s.

The Bubble going up, 1975.

C. M. Victor Harding
Squash

Canadian Men's
Doubles
   1978, 1981, 1987

U.S. Men's Doubles
   1977, 1981, 1983

Canadian Mixed
Doubles
   1982, 1983, 1984,
   1985, 1987. 1988

U.S. Mixed Doubles
   1989

Canadian Men's
Veterans Doubles
(40+)
   1991, 1992

World Masters Men's
Doubles
   1985

World Veterans
Doubles (40+)
   1994

Member Canadian
Men's ISRF Team
   1977

Canadian Mixed
Veteran Doubles
   1995, 1999

U.S. Veteran Doubles
(40+)
   1999

There were Tuesday evenings, round robins, after school, parent and child, and weekend play. A badminton tournament was arranged in 1978 for "seasoned" players. Ann Richmond and John Pinkham, who had won the mixed doubles twenty-five years earlier, captured the title again. The name of Westcott featured once more — Bev Westcott and Budd Porter won the Men's Doubles, and Pam Westcott with Ann Richmond won the Ladies' Doubles. Pam Davidson won the Ladies' Singles. Thanks to the work of Mary Knowles and Jimmy Stuart to rejuvenate badminton, activity continued to increase.

In 1978 Derek Bocquet was honoured for twenty-five years with the club and given a trip to Bermuda. It was calculated that he had given 47,240 lessons in those twenty-five years. Sandy Morgan was appointed a teaching pro, available for lessons in all racquet sports, and for round robins and clinics. Someone discovered that in 1953 Derek had given his first lesson at the B&R to John Bassett Sr. and his second to Sandy Morgan, and that twenty-six years later Sandy Morgan, had given his first lesson to John Bassett Jr, as teaching pro.

And then there was platform tennis, or "paddle."

> "The informality of platform tennis is so great. You get out there on Saturday mornings. You don't have to have a match arranged. You just go out there. Four go out and then you have a cup of coffee, and then another four go out, or maybe two of the same. You can play in any weather all winter as long as you get the snow shovelled off. It's informal. It's outside and it's here to stay."
> *Jock Maynard.*

> Platform tennis, a form of tennis designed for the outdoors in winter, was played in New York as early as 1928 by keen sportsmen who were looking for a strenuous but social outdoor activity. They built a wooden platform over a rocky area, hoping to play deck tennis or badminton, and when this proved unworkable, they took short-handled racquets, or paddles, and a sponge rubber ball, and created a new sport. The ball bounced readily off the tight wire mesh that surrounded the deck, ensuring long rallies and a rigorous workout. There was a non-skid surface made from crushed walnut shells glued to the deck. Aluminum or steel courts, with heating beneath and night lighting, were later improvements. By the 1970s there were 4,000 paddle courts in the U.S. The game was played in informal sportswear of any colour.
>
> The game came to Nova Scotia, then Montreal, and by 1972 it reached Toronto where paddle enthusiasts Elijah Jones, a Virginian who had moved to Toronto's Forest Hill, and the Ferguson and Stulac families, became the hub of platform activity. Both built private courts in their gardens. Jones founded the Canadian Platform Tennis Association and Ferguson the Kingsway Club; one Stulac son has coached at the B&R.

Some of the Forest Hill group were B&R members. Peter Gordon brought a proposal to the board, and it agreed to put a temporary platform tennis court on the boards over the tennis courts as an experiment for one year. It was thought that paddle would take some of the pressure off the tennis courts. A second-hand platform tennis court was purchased for $18,900, and installed in its current location. Then the board was told that a platform tennis court needed a warm-up hut. President Peter Stewart and others sought out what they saw as a simple hut but, as Peter says, "We got back from the summer and all of a sudden the city came at us with their fire regulations and the cost almost tripled." When this estimate was presented at the annual

Platform competitors Nancy Doherty, Pam O'Rorke, Mary Gordon, Mary Harnett, in 1979.

Opening day of platform tennis at the B&R, 1977.

Enjoying the new "Paddle" court. Skee and Heather McClelland.

Peter B. Hatcher
Platform Tennis

Canadian Men's
Doubles
1974, 1983, 1985

Squash

Canadian Men's
Doubles (50+)
1992, 1993

Canadian Men's
Veteran Singles
Hardball (40+)
1986

Canadian Men's
Singles Hardball
(45+)
1990, 1991

Canadian Men's
Singles Hardball
(50+)
1992, 1993

Martin Walker
Platform Tennis

Canadian Men's
Doubles
1974, 1975

> "Voting day was our best day. No booze was sold on voting day so everyone stocked up their locker. By six o'clock everyone in the back rooms was squiffed. Voting day was our greatest party."
>
> *Chink Fleming*

meeting it caused quite a stir, bringing comments from keen platform players and from those opposed to the idea and its cost. Then Gordon Fisher rose and, in his calm, reasoned manner, said that there were clearly members who enjoyed paddle tennis. Why not let them go ahead and see what they could make of it. The motion was passed. Peter recalls Gordon's words. " He took the arm wrestling out of it." The

> "Before the last renovation the men's locker room had a small number of full-sized lockers, the kind that you can hang a coat in, six foot high. They were much coveted. You could put your name on a list and hope that you lived long enough to get one. Norman Longmore, who was a boiler room stoker first class, talked to me a lot. We had the Navy in common and I guess he thought I had befriended him. He came to me one day and said, 'How would you like to have a large locker?' I turned down the chance to jump the line, but that's how things were run then. A sort of back-of-the-envelope operation."
>
> *George Currie*

hut was built during the fall and winter, when the bubble kept it hidden. When the bubble came down the hut was instantly named Peter's Palace or the Taj Mahal. An additional court was eventually approved in 1980. The B&R paddle court was the tenth in Toronto.

The first Canadian tournament was held in 1974, a national men's doubles competition. Peter Hatcher, who brought enthusiasm and prowess to the fledgling group, and his partner, Martin Walker, won the Elijah Jones trophy. The following year women's doubles, mixed and junior were included. More than 120 teams participated. Among early B&R Canadian champions were Chuck Baird, Norma Baird, Nancy Doherty, Mary Gordon, Ruth Grant, Doug

Fred Gundy, "Mr. Back-Room."

Grant, Pam O'Rorke, Peter Hatcher, and Martin Walker. Nancy Doherty and Pam O'Rorke were acknowledged the best around the B&R for years and active in competition. Soon there was a full complement of women's house leagues and club players competing against the Bay Street Racquet Club and the Kingsway Club.

Then, in 1970, a trophy was donated for another major club sport. No activities at the B&R have had more devoted supporters than dominoes and backgammon. The Members' Lounge, where the concentration was intense,

The indefatigable Ernie Whelpton with Gat Taylor, in the 1970s.

Absolute silence. At the table left to right, Humphrey Gilbert, Bob Gaby, Don Redfern.
Standing, John Shields and Larry Heisey.

Four Saturday morning players. John Waldie, Bruce Taylor, Peter Hatcher, Phil MacDonnell.

Mary Gordon
Platform Tennis

Canadian Ladies
Doubles
1976

Ruth Grant
Platform Tennis

Canadian Mixed
Doubles
1976

Canadian Ladies
Doubles
1976

Doug Grant
Platform Tennis

Canadian Mixed
Doubles
1976

Pamela H. O'Rorke
Platform Tennis

Canadian Ladies
Doubles
1981, 1982, 1983,
1984

Charles F. Baird
Platform Tennis

Canadian Men's
Doubles
1981, 1982, 1983,
1984

Tennis

Canadian Masters
Doubles (60+)
1985, 1986

Norma Baird
Platform Tennis

Canadian Ladies
Doubles
1983, 1987

was the scene of many battles that attracted a gallery of spectators. "You had to get there early," says Humphrey Gilbert, veteran dominoes player and champion on a number of occasions, "or you wouldn't be able to play on a Saturday. When the tournament came around there was a huge entry list." Competition was for the J.A. Hanley trophy, a unique award that is on display in the Members' Lounge above the dominoes table. It is awarded at an annual dinner. And over the years there was one dominoes player who was acknowledged as the best. A tribute was paid to him by Larry Heisey who gathered the dominoes players together in his honour. "Fred Gundy," says Humphrey, "was the dean of the dominoes group."

In March 1978 the first B&R newsletter announced

> "Who could ever forget the unforgettable Ernie Whelpton? He was probably the most competitive member we ever had as well as the fittest for his age. To be sure, he sometimes became confused as to the number of bounces the ball had taken, but what a competitor! On one occasion his tennis doubles partner was aced down the centre line; Ernie dashed across the court and returned the serve before it hit the stop netting. He maintained that it was perfectly legal, as his partner had been unable to reach it! But perhaps his finest hour came when, having just lost a match to Paul Henderson, he complained he had been unfairly distracted by the sun reflecting off the top of Paul's head."
>
> *Derek Bocquet*

> "I was playing doubles with Harry Fauquier as my partner. I was on the court but I wasn't allowed to hit the ball. I said to Harry, 'This is no fun for me. I'm not getting any exercise except walking out, changing ends and picking up the ball.' But we had a match the likes of which shouldn't be told. We were playing against Chris Ondaatje and Doug Grant. They had won the first set six-love. They were leading in the second set five-love. They were trouncing us. Then two little kids came down and stood looking at us. Chris said, 'Move away please, I can't see the ball.' They moved away but they came back. He got so upset he couldn't serve the ball. They lost the next game. We finally tied them and then beat them seven to five. I will always remember that tennis game."
>
> *Chink Fleming*

that Vic Harding had won the Ontario Singles Hardball squash over the previous winner, Jay Gillespie, who had earlier won the Ontario Doubles. There was an article about squash balls — the hardball (70+) used in the narrow U.S. courts versus the softball (yellow dot). There was an enticement to the dining room, for the Saturday night special — five courses for $10.50 with filet mignon and lobster — and the family buffet dinner on Wednesdays, $6.00 per person, children under 12 half price. The backgammon and dominoes finalists dinner was announced. The newsletter has been a fine addition, keeping members more fully informed about club activities.

Not One But Two.

Mary and George Heintzman, Roland Michener and Hope Salmond, in 1967.

A little-known fact that emerged from the research for this book is that the Badminton and Racquet Club can count two Governors-General on its past membership lists.

Vincent Massey was the eighteenth Governor-General since Confederation. From 1921 to 1925 he was president of Massey-Harris Company, which grew from Daniel Massey's farm-implement company into an international corporation. He joined the army and eventually worked for the war committee of cabinet. Then, in 1926, Mackenzie King appointed him Canada's first minister to the United States. An original member of the B&R, he wrote from Washington to George Blackstock and the board in 1927 tendering his resignation due to his new posting. The board replied, asking him to reconsider and accept Honorary Membership while he and Mrs. Massey were in Washington. He accepted. In 1946 he was named High Commissioner to Britain. Some years later he had the honour of becoming Canada's first native-born Governor-General, a post he filled from 1952 to 1959.

Daniel Roland Michener loved his racquet sports. A Toronto lawyer, MPP from 1945 to 1948 with three years in cabinet, then MP for Toronto St. Paul's from 1953 to 1962, he was made Speaker of the House. Then an appointment as High Commissioner to India followed, and finally the post of Governor-General in 1967. Michener was known for his dedication to fitness. In his ninetieth year he said in an interview that his daily routine included fourteen minutes of the Canadian Armed Forces exercises, including push-ups, then a work-out on his rowing machine. He played tennis three times a week and "If I was out on a big bender the night before and didn't feel like getting up in the morning, I'd force myself to get up and exercise vigorously. A long-time member of the Toronto Lawn Tennis Club, he was made an honorary life member of the B&R in 1974 and enjoyed the facilities of the club.

The Car Barns Have Another Upgrade

"'Now then,' Derek said to me after a lesson, "would you like me to remodel your game completely or would you like to keep playing the kind of tennis you have been playing all your life?' I decided to not go for the remodelling. He told it as it was."
Skee McClelland

"I think one of the great strengths of the club is the way the board is constructed, with twelve people each in a three-year term. Four go off each year, which gives continuity and change and prevents self-perpetuating. With 2,600 members there is a tremendous cadre of talented people that you can feed into the board."
Skee McClelland

"The survey in 1986 showed tremendous support for fitness. The board found it hard to believe. It was a surprise when members put their action where their mouths were."
Peter Townley

"Bill Munro and I were of the same opinion. The key thing was getting women on the board. When we did the ladies' committee disbanded. After all those years it was very simple in the end."
Don Redfern

What became a decade of controversy began with discussions between the board and the ladies' committee on that perennial subject, women on the board. The idea had been rejected many times since it was first raised in 1934 when Norman Seagram politely told them that the "right kind of man" would not serve if there were women at the table.

Valerie Guest had written in the mid-seventies on behalf of the ladies' committee, thanking the board for their co-operation in the past year and reminding them that the committee still felt strongly regarding representation on the board. The result was that the subject was aired and communication was improved. Three women, — Elizabeth Telfer, Maggie Corcoran, and Ann Cooper — were invited to attend a board meeting and the entire committee was included in dinner after the meeting. The head of the ladies' committee gave a report for the first time at the 1976 annual meeting. Her committee was introduced, and all were asked to stand.

In June, 1980, the first Past and Present Ladies' Committee Dinner was organized by Maggie Corcoran, Mary Heighington, Annabelle Heintzman, Mary Godfrey, Joan Stewart and Elizabeth Telfer. Extensive detective work was required to track down candidates. Joan Stewart created a listing to record years served. There was an unexpectedly high attendance of sixty-five women, some of whom had travelled great distances to be there. Some, as Maggie's report stated, "were on the committee so long ago that no one knew who they were." The highlight of the evening was hearing three speakers from past committees who gave vignettes from years gone by.

The first was Willa Glassco, who was on the committee in the late 1940s. Along with Alice (Allie-Mo) Wickett, her task was to decorate the new lounge "from the bottom up — curtains, rugs, chintz and paintings." They did it for $2,500 and for another $25 they bought all the Christmas decorations. Then there was the Heintzman piano, a beautiful grand purchased for $700 with the old upright as a trade-in. Willa mentioned that, as ever, there were complaints. "The highlight of the complaints we had to deal with was the request to have the WC doors lengthened. We were very embarrassed to have to bring this before the men's committee, believe it or not, and blushingly we did so, with success, and the doors were lengthened by four inches — was it our blush?

We played badminton….and were inspired by players like Mrs. Coke and Mrs. Boone and others who played on and on — how wise they were! Old age comes to us all. I have reached that delectable time and all I can say is keep fit and keep up your interests and enthusiasms."

The next speaker was Betsy Stowe, who quipped that when she had been asked to speak to a group referred to as "former ladies," it led her to wonder what they were now. She read some minutes from the 1970s and told of the "earth-shaking matters" they were called upon to deal with, petty pilfering of soap, hair spray, shower caps, mirrors. "It is rather careless of people to roll up such things in their dirty laundry!"

She recalled the year they tied Christmas balls around "that horse in the centre of the bar," but quickly removed them when they saw the smirk on the bartender's face, and realized that "we had decorated the iron horse more than we meant to."

Lou Anne Cassels took the stage and regaled the group. She recalled the "bright and gifted Billy Wilder into whose care the enlightened board chose to entrust the ultra challenge of the second coming of the old car barn." And "the vivacious Mary Kent" who could be seen on B&R shopping expeditions "in confident and profound consultations with various antique store dealers." They all "admired her decisiveness until they realized that she was shopping for her own house."

She remembered the time the ladies' committee was invited to join the board for a dinner meeting and "got tarted up with high heels, pearls, and Chanel Number Five." When the men were late arriving, they decided to start the cocktail hour without them. After dinner with wine, followed by brandy and liqueurs, someone proposed they play tennis and "the usually controlled Annabelle Heintzman" could be seen on a court "behaving like overcooked spaghetti, with a Cheshire cat smile. She was waving her racquet aimlessly at a nearby ball" while her male partner leapt over the net to congratulate the opponents, "but sadly hooked his toe in the top of the net" and "nearly became faceless." The conclusion for all was that they "loved the place."

In September 1980 the practice of having the chairman of the ladies' committee sit in on each board meeting was initiated, but she could neither vote nor attend the dinner following the meeting. Then in 1981 Mary Heighington, as chairman of the ladies' committee, was allowed to sit in on all board meetings and join the men for dinner. The following year the vice-president was included. One of the best submissions on this fifty-year-old subject came from Esther Eastmure. She submitted four points to the board: female representation at the board level had been repeatedly requested over the years; the senior ladies' membership almost equalled that of the men; there was an equal single membership fee; and, she concluded, "I believe women are equal — different — but equal." She asked that the views of the membership be sought in a questionnaire. Request declined. It was easy to lobby a questionnaire. The ball was back in the women's court again. It was possible that they were preparing for a slam shot.

Recognizing this state of affairs in 1982 the president, Bill Munro, tackled the issue head-on at the most significant forum, the dinner for the past presidents and directors. Bill remembers setting about planning his words carefully. "I was more uptight preparing for that than any other speech I have ever made." He added, "If the wives had heard some of the statements made by their husbands on this subject over the years there would have been havoc at home."

The motion put forward was that: "It is the recommendation of the present Board to the incoming Board, that nominations be put forward for election to the Board next December, 1983, to included a minimum of two ladies." His expectations for a raucous debate were cut short. "Clair Balfour stood up and said 'Bill, you are absolutely right. It's time we did it.' There was not a comment. Not a question."

At the next annual meeting Annabelle Heintzman and Nancy Doherty were elected, the first two women members of the board. Bill Munro said that there was strong support for this move, with a few notable exceptions, who would remain nameless, and that he "gained considerable comfort from the fact that in taking this action we would not be creating a divisive situation in the club. I do not wish to labour this point but as full fee-paying and very active members of this club, the ladies are entitled to be represented on the board and no sustainable argument can be put forward in support of maintaining our historical position."

Annabelle Heintzman, one of the first two women on the board, with Anne McLeod, the last chairman of the ladies' committee.

The ladies' committee would no longer be necessary in the same form. Women would have equal representation on the house and courts committees, and the two women on the board would be the ladies' membership committee. A new committee would be formed to take care of special events such as the Christmas dance, the children's Christmas party, fitness classes and bridge. Members of these committees would be women, and their chair would report directly to the board. Ann Cooper was elected chairman of special events with Judy Korthals as vice-chairman.

A final ladies' committee meeting took place, with a report by Anne McLeod, the last ladies' chairman. She said, "I would like to think that our contribution has been positive enough that it is not only a sign of the times that women be elected to the board, but that we have proven that we are indeed more than decorative fixtures." And, as Bill Munro said, "If we hadn't done it there would have been a palace revolt."

Only slightly less controversial were the endeavors of the art committee. Don Redfern, chairman, got knowledgeable people on the committee — Gay Evans, Pam Gibson, Emmy Lind and Jane Zeidler. It was formed to "acquire for the Club a collection of works of art of medium value created for the most part by Canadians." Once the collection was established trading or sale would continue without any additional cash input. Art was a hot subject.

"We were in a tennis tournament, John Weir and I against Fred Thompson and his partner. I made a shot that I thought was a point and the winner. I turned to John to congratulate him on our victory, when the ball came whipping by. I had been standing right in Johnny's way so he couldn't see the return shot."
Bill Munro.

"If we ever get women on the board they should be beautiful but dumb."
Absolutely anonymous.

> "When the invitation to our first Past and Present Directors' dinner came I said 'Nancy, the invitation says black tie. Why don't we go in black tie?' So we got black sequined jackets and black trousers, white shirt, and black tie.... There are such a variety of issues to be dealt with that women absolutely have a place on the board. I think women are very good at getting to the point and getting the job done. When I was appointed to the board a member said to me, 'Well, if we have to have women on the board it might as well be you!'"
> — *Annabelle Heintzman*

The controversial painting, "Ladies of the Night." A Dutch "hooker," a small boat, in the background.

Badminton and Racquet Club is in my opinion primarily an athletic club, secondly a comfortable social facility, and thirdly an art gallery. Some of the paintings move around the club more quickly than a number of our athletes."

All got a shock when, in November 1981, it was discovered that A.Y. Jackson's "A Winter Morning" had been stolen. It had been purchased for $100 in 1934 and was worth $30,000 in 1981. The insurer paid for the painting and it was decided that the club should not keep paintings worth more than $3,000. Then, in October 1984, it was reported that a Jeffrey Armstrong painting had been stolen. The club's collection became a hot topic, no more so than when it was decided to clean the old painting of two women purchased for that collection many years before by Dolly Proctor and Gerald Larkin. Don Redfern, president in 1983, remembers the incident well. "The humorous part of the year involved the art committee. We had the painting "Ladies of the Night" cleaned. Then we could see they were on a wharf with a small Dutch ship in the background. It was ironic that this type of ship was called a "hooker." This piece of information was around the club in a day!

The end of an era came in 1984 with the retirement of Derek Bocquet. He was feted with a dinner and made an honorary playing member of the club. His successor was Sandy Morgan, who had been a B&R member some years earlier, at which time he partnered John Foy to win a junior tennis championship. Sandy had been a pro at The

Members had strong preferences and, in traditional B&R style, did not hesitate to express opinions. Tony Wells summed up the problem in his inimitable way. "The

Sandy Morgan running a children's clinic with the Taj Mahal and one platform tennis court in the background.

Paul Dunning

Waterloo Tennis Club in the summers and The Kitchener-Waterloo Racquet Club in the winters. He earned certification at the highest level in Canada for tennis coaching, as well as advanced levels in badminton. Sandy was taken on at the B&R as a teaching professional but returned to Kitchener-Waterloo in 1986. It was in Sandy's time as pro that Paul Dunning came to the B&R. Paul was from the University of Waterloo and the University of Toronto, a physical education grad from the early 1980s who had experience as squash pro at a downtown club (now called Bloor Valley). Paul has won the Canadian Singles Hardball championship three times.

Then, the unanimous choice of the search committee, Eleanor O'Gorman came to the club as sports director after eleven years at the Granite Club, where she had been senior tennis and squash professional. Eleanor met the members for the first time at a Wimbledon dinner on

"There are so many talented people in the club. When I was president I had a board that could match any corporate board that you could name. It is fun to work with people like that. The meetings were good and crisp."
Bill Munro

Frank C. Dimock
Tennis

Canadian Men's Masters Doubles (60+)
1985a

the finals day, with a replay on video and her accompanying comments.

Eleanor, who had spent eight years teaching school in Winnipeg, where she was a recognized athlete, came to Toronto in the early 1970s and immediately found a network of Winnipegers and sports associates to set her on the right track. This led to her first position at the Mayfair Club.

Eleanor O'Gorman.

> "Whether they are national champions or not we don't care, the children should love it. And they will bring out their parents."
> *Eleanor O'Gorman*

"I had a good winter there," she recalls, "then Ken Sinclair, whom I had met when I was president of the Manitoba Tennis Association, and we had the Canadian tennis championships, said there was a job at the Cricket Club for the summer. After that the Granite Club needed someone for a squash position. I had met George Mansfield when he used to tour across Canada. The Granite had a great number of women so I went there as an assistant squash professional." When the tennis and squash pros left, Eleanor ran both those departments. "Then I found that Sandy was leaving the B&R so I came down for an interview. When I walked in I knew every person in the room — Tony Wells had been in Winnipeg, Sue Behan and I had played a lot of squash, I had met John Pinkham in squash — and I ended up here."

Tennis Canada was just beginning to develop the action method, which Eleanor was using, teaching by getting the feel. Looking back over her sixteen years she notes, "Any changes I made were strategic goal-setting — eight in a clinic this year and sixteen next. The badminton clinics for juniors were four weeks in November and four weeks in February. We have been working away at it with an eight-week program. Paul has worked very hard at the basics and getting the juniors to know each other. We had a nice letter from a member who said it is wonderful to see her children come in and run to a friend. There were clinics in the winter every day after school and some training for the elite Canadian championships. We have a separate category for junior members whose parents are not members of the club. It helps to bring in people with a passion for the sport. They are there because they really like it. They understand there is no nonsense. We have struggled with the concept of depth. Two or three is no good. Depth is ten or more for variety."

Cynthia Mitchell and Penny McLeod, outstanding junior tennis players in the 1980s.

As the end of one era had come with the retirement of Derek Bocquet, the end of another came with the loss of Norman Longmore. It was time for his retirement but the club had been his life for the last twenty years and the break was very hard. A retirement party was planned and the date was set, to take place ten days after his last working day. And so, his last full day put in, he left the club. It was with utter disbelief late that same day that staff and members heard he had gone home and suffered a heart attack and died. He was replaced by Pat McCann, who had been general manager of the Scarboro Golf and Country Club for four years.

It was time to look to the future and improvements again. A future planning committee had been set up in the seventies with Ian Stewart as chairman. In November 1980, after the needs of the club to the year

The sixtieth anniversary dance. David Kent, Bill Heintzman, Jim McLeod, Walter Pady, George Currie, John Evans, Mary Kent, Gay Evans, Annabelle Heintzman, Mary Corcoran, Daphne Currie, Anne McLeod, Lynn Pady.

2000 were discussed, and a report, based on a survey, was tabled by Barnard and Associates after consultation with president Bill Heintzman, and members Peter Townley and Val Stock.

It was decided not to proceed with enlarging the tennis facilities, to add an additional paddle tennis court, to convert squash courts four and five to international size, and to carry out a feasibility study regarding future international squash courts. At the 1980 annual meeting, the international squash courts were approved.

The terms of the Year 2000 Task Force, initiated in 1985, and chaired by returning director, Peter Barnard, at the request of president Alan Watson, were wide-ranging — to look at the needs of the members, the facilities, the possibility of relocating the club, and short-term needs. The Task Force members were Gord Cheesbrough, Doug Grant, Annabelle Heintzman, Steve Irwin, Bill Munro, Kathy Vernon, and Susan Wright. Concerns soon emerged. Since 1965 the membership had grown by one third, yet the courts facilities were the same, except for the addition of two platform tennis courts. Members were using the courts and keeping active in racquet sports, particularly doubles tennis, well into their eighties. An architect would prepare plans, incorporating future needs. Soon the Task Force committee had twenty members and several sub-committees, representing the broad range of member interests.

As part of the work of the Task Force, a membership survey was done in 1986 and it showed that most wanted to keep the club at its present size, (2,500 members, a zero growth policy, with a substantial waiting list). Members thought that tennis court availability was too restricted, and that a four-court bubble would be popular, as would a satellite tennis facility no more than a mile away. A fitness facility was in demand, as was an informal sports lounge with a snack bar. There was a plea for more daytime parking and the first mention of baby-sitting. The club's younger members were keen about the planned expansion, especially in the fitness area. Their ideas represented the future and were very much family-oriented. A drop-off in the 25 to 35 age group was foreseen if their interests were not taken into account.

"It was time to orchestrate a long-range plan for the club," explained Peter Barnard, "so for the two years before my presidency I was involved in a broad process. We set up groups of different ages. By the time I became president it was time to get the plan accepted by the membership. We had taken a fairly new look at the club, everything from its demographics to comparisons with different clubs — their facilities versus ours. And so that was the context of my presidency. It was time to rethink the previous adage that this was a place that never spent money. I had a very good board and they were solidly behind this idea. The long-range plan was not just a physical thing, it was a modernization of the club."

John S. Boynton
Squash

Canadian Mixed Doubles
1986

Canadian Men's Veterans Doubles (40+)
1990, 1993

Canadian Men's Doubles
1997, 1998

The report of Task Force 2000 was tabled. The price tag would be $3 million. It was presented to the board, then the past and present directors, former ladies' committee members, and to a members' information meeting. Eight hundred members attended. Discussion at the annual meeting was lively. Options were explored to increase play for the ever-expanding tennis group. Tennis raised above the parking area? — Too expensive. Parking under the badminton hall? — $750,000, so offsite parking would be more reasonable. It was recommended that a search be made for a four-court facility within walking distance of the club. Some wanted winter fitness only, but other club experience was that an all-year facility was better. Two more international squash courts were desirable. There would be an assessment of $600 for seniors with membership of longer than two years.

Requests were made for a deferred decision — some said we should be looking for a window onto St. Clair Avenue or Yonge Street; they thought the club should consider moving elsewhere instead of sitting on its limited site. Fran's restaurant was coming up for sale. David Higginbotham, finance chairman, said that if the property became available, funds could be raised, and that the club had first option there. The motion for deferral was narrowly defeated on the basis that delay would create more indecision. An alternative plan was proposed, which had some considerable support, but the Task Force said they had considered the matters proposed and they were too expensive. When the initial vote on the Task Force report was put to the members at the annual meeting in 1986, the decision was to proceed. It was made after much debate, with a vote of 211 to 143. "They spilled out of the room," says Peter Barnard. "The result was that we brought the club into the modern world, but there was opposition to fitness, lots of opposition to baby-sitting, and lots of opposition to a fairly substantial investment. One key was the new sports bar with a concentration of activity, bringing sporting activities together with a place to see them."

A subcommittee, called the Real Estate Opportunity Monitoring Committee, was formed. Steve Irwin, John de Pencier, and Bill Munro would keep in touch with other property owners about developments in the St. Clair and Yonge area and become familiar with information about all properties adjoining the B&R with a view to obtaining increased parking, property frontage, extra space for tennis, and a possible frontage on St. Clair Avenue.

In February, 1987, when the expansion was still under debate, a seemingly ideal proposal came forward that could be incorporated in the final plans. The club learned that the CNR wanted to sell its tennis club on Cottingham Street, but its present members could not offer enough. It consisted of two buildings, and four Har-Tru courts. It was within the physical range defined by the Task Force 2000. It would provide extra facilities for

"The entire financial future of the world is forecast with blinding accuracy in the men's locker room."
Derek Bocquet

Construction, 1989.

A few members and guests go for the stonewashed and shredded jeans look. It would be appreciated if members would save this fashion statement for other occasions.
Board Minutes, January, 1991

junior programs and tournaments, and there was parking space available. It seemed a dream. It turned out to be something of a nightmare.

The price was $1.7 million. In the first year there would be capital items of up to half a million (repairs to buildings, court lighting, bubble, fences). The operating cost for the first year would be $124,000. Elsie Falconer, Bill Munro, Peter Barnard and Doug Haldenby were empowered to negotiate with the CNR and meet with the local community organization around the CNR club. It was decided that the B&R would rent the premises for the summer if our offer to purchase was turned down. A deal was negotiated with the CNR that required a deposit of $100,000 and, if the plan did not meet with the approval of the B&R membership, $50,000 of that amount would be forfeited.

The CNR approved the B&R offer, with the proviso that the CNR club members had asked for a meeting to ascertain if limited playing time would be available to them. That meeting turned out to be hostile, as local ratepayers expressed fears about everything from traffic, parking, and the noise of construction, to lighting and accessibility of play to their current membership.

What followed was an offer by the B&R to rent the facility for three years for $85,000 and for a second three-year period at $90,000 if the courts were getting sufficient use. This was accepted by the CNR president. At the same time the club's offer to purchase would stand for six years. The executive of the community organization approved the arrangements. A special meeting was held for B&R members in May, 1987, at which, Peter Barnard recalls, there must have been 1000 in attendance. At this point political pressure had become intense, instigated by a few local residents who were members of the CNR club, and aided and abetted by those in a position to slow down or stop proceedings. The matter reached the federal cabinet.

In the end the CNR refused to honour their deal with the B&R. The whole affair was summed up at the 1987 annual meeting by Peter Barnard. "Unfortunately the CNR board delayed ratifying the deal under political pressure, and the small group of CNR club members abutting the club property turned to the media to activate further opposition. The media seemed disinterested in our side of the story…. Our opponents….resorted to the media with deliberate intention to harm our Club's reputation…. From my perspective this situation has been very much like a tennis match I'd like to forget. We've lost a tie-breaker in the fifth set, having had three match points against an opponent who cheats and an umpire who sways with the will of the crowd." He concluded, "Thank you for the opportunity to serve you and the club. I am now looking forward to some time to enjoy it." His remarks received a standing ovation.

Meanwhile, as this saga continued, plans for the major renovation were moving along. A revised plan would be drawn up for member viewing without the CNR club acquisition included. The chairman of the finance committee, Elsie Falconer, presented alternate plans for financing — a combination of assessment, an increase in annual fees and a substantial increase in

Peter Barnard. Time to enjoy the club again.

entrance fees, or the club could mortgage the property on a twenty-five year amortization pay-back and increase annual dues by $200 to cover the debt service. These plans were later revised so there was a $300 assessment for 1987 and 1988 for senior and family members. Construction would begin in 1989, and the club would be closed from April to October. Other clubs would extend playing privileges to B&R members. The budget for renovations was projected to be between $3 million and $3.5 million but this did not include fees or decoration costs, water, drainage or sanitary costs.

Then, in 1988, as construction was about to begin, the possibility of Frans being for sale finally came up. The questions were — how would this affect B&R renovations? What would the members think if the club did not pursue this possibility? It was decided to go ahead with club renovations. Fran was more interested in leasing than selling his property and put a price of $6 million on buying, which the club viewed as over-priced and beyond our capacity. It was decided to keep in touch. The budget for renovations was taking off — $3.5 million plus contingencies came to $4.05 million, plus interior details of $760,000, plus permits, bubble, computerization, fees to the engineer, construction manager, and interior decorator. The total project, after unexpected surprises found in renovating an old building, mushroomed to $5.9 million. But the treasurer, Doug Bassett, expressed the opinion at the 1989 annual meeting that, "although the club will have, in my opinion, a debt in the amount of $3 million, there is no serious cause for concern." A loan would be negotiated. Further assessments were planned. The entrance fee went to $10,000.

In spite of major problems, the closing produced some interesting events. The Closing Down party was a huge success, particularly the tours of his and hers locker rooms. Other events took place outside the club — dinner theatre, trips to Stratford and Niagara-on-the-Lake, and the U.S. Open. The club became events-oriented. Club members enjoyed privileges at sixteen prominent area clubs. Staff dispersed, placed with the help of secretary manager Pat McCann and several members. Maria went to Islington Golf and Country Club, the maitre d' to the Hunt Club. Murph and Ralph retired, but returned part time. Eleanor moved the pro shop to the platform tennis hut. Two courts would be in use. Paul went to the Toronto Lawn Tennis Club.

When the dust settled the club had enlarged men's and ladies' locker rooms, improved food service throughout the main floor, created a new informal dining room and a new fitness facility. There was covered and heated access to all courts in winter. There were washrooms upstairs. The Blue Room was improved. There was a new private dining area, new office space, an elevator from the basement to the second floor, a new ladies' lounge, a new sports lounge, and international squash courts. The staff returned and everyone was welcomed back with an Open House January 21, 1990. And the first reaction to the fitness came in. Even before it opened 375 members had shown a commitment to this exciting new facility. Peter Barnard sums up the reconstruction era at a ten-year perspective by saying, "It was not a quiet time, but the board was strong."

The new issues in the wind for the nineties would require new attitudes for significant new lifestyles — a totally unexpected surge of interest in fitness, talk of non-smoking areas, baby-sitting facilities, a new dress code. And, of course, there was the debt.

A Family Club for the Nineties

"'Members must recognize the necessity to use weights to keep fit. Weights are the key. We would like to attract older people. It slows down the decline. But you know it is easier to lift a martini than a weight."

    Milan Jablonsky

"Introducing minimum house accounts now would be the equivalent of bringing in a sledgehammer to knock in a small nail. The accompanying shock would be far greater than the slight success."

    David Higginbotham,
    as finance chairman, advocating
    rejection of this unpopular idea.

"One year when the budget was really bad there was a smoking issue. The adamant smoke-free people were at loggerheads with the smoking people and nobody paid attention to financial matters. And then there were many of the older members who had been so much opposed to the fitness facility thinking it was far too avant garde for the B&R. They were to be seen a couple of months later up there working out. People are very interesting."

    Sue Sisam

"I have only been a member for five years but I have represented the B&R in everything from national to local championships and there is no doubt that this is a club a lot of people envy. When I came here there was a waiting list to join but it was pretty clear to me that this was the club that I wanted to join. I have put up a number of friends for membership since I joined here. People love to come and play here. We host really good events. There are only a handful of clubs in the country that can do that properly, certainly for squash and badminton."

    David Stevenson

"There is no doubt about the reputation this club has. People envy us."

    Gill Evans

"Murphy was great. He was a grump with a gruff side but he had a sense of humour."

Sara Adamson

"I am excited about the sports activity in all areas of the club from the youngest juniors to the stalwart players in their eighties. I feel that the place right now is just pushing at the seams. The walls should be rubber."

Eleanor O'Gorman

"We have so many older men still playing and it is wonderful. You go into the sports lounge and there are four men who have just played. They are sitting with their heads together. You would think they were plotting a murder but they are having a great time together."

Hope Salmond

"It took a lot of calls to arrange a game. Five minutes later someone would cancel out. It wasn't easy. Some would say I don't want to play with him or him. That's the time they ended up with each other."

Murphy

Some presidencies, due to the initiatives of the day, pass with only minor problems to control, a steady steering of the ship. Others have a daily feast of issues on the table. The presidencies from the late 1980s to the mid-1990s had a banquet. But the same period, as well, became a time of proud accomplishments, exciting changes, and the use of a vibrant facility bursting with activity. There was a seesaw between the high points and the important deliberations at the board table.

The operative word for the succession of presidents and boards in the first half of the nineties was "clean-up." The beautiful new facilities were being used with gusto, but there were major financial problems to be dealt with and a

Still stalwart players in 1992. Murray Ross, Jack Crean, Bill Parker, Harry Dawson.

few deficiencies in the design to be addressed. Letters came to the board — a plus rating for the sports lounge with its good visibility of tennis and badminton, and the fitness room with its individually designed programs. The front entrance did not receive a passing grade. Designed as a transition space from the driveway to the inner part of the club, it seemed cold and uninviting. The Trophy Room informality and openness was adopted slowly, then utilized heartily in time. As Skee McClelland said, "You can see the whole life of the club when you are sitting there. I love it." And, in the wind, were other concepts for the B&R to deal with — changes in sporting preferences, an appropriate dress code, "gender equality in club space," baby-sitting, non-smoking, new life-styles.

But first to get the financial house in order. Skee McClelland, the first president to inherit the clean-up, wrote a letter to the members in May, 1990. He set the tone by telling them it would be best if they were sitting down when they read it! The total costs incurred for the renovations were $6.8 million. He continued "The project expanded beyond the plan. It was originally intended to work only in a limited area of the property and to leave other areas untouched. As the project proceeded, problems encountered in the building, mostly of an electrical and mechanical nature dealing with life safety or fire code regulations, expanded the project into all areas of the club. Now we must pay for it." There were resignations;

At the opening of the Bistro in the Blue Room.
Budd Porter, David Higginbotham, Bev Westcott,
Skee McClelland, with Calum Grieg.

there was a downturn in the economy; there were assessments. One thing led to another. "The more assessments, the more people you lose. Changes send people through the roof," Skee said. "The members got sick of my letters. So did my secretary. When I said to her that we had to do another B&R letter she would say, 'What now?' Everything was new — the sports lounge concept, day care, the survey, the plan, interest groups. Unanimity was pretty scarce."

The bottom line was a debt of $4 million. The front lobby needed to be altered. Money needed to be spent on the Trophy Room, the Blue Room, artwork, draperies and furnishings, architectural changes. Interest on the debt, said

> "Our attitude towards having children at the club has changed. There used to be grudging tolerance of children but we are more of a family club than we were twenty years ago. It is a societal change, a shared responsibility, now they are accepted."
> George Currie

the treasurer, Warren Moysey, was $40,000 a month. The obvious move was to deal with the problem as soon as possible. A special meeting was held in June, 1990, at which Warren Moysey put a proposal: the assessment would be $1,000 per member. But the plan was defeated. It was too hard on the younger and older members. A new proposal was acceptable with a choice of semi-annual protracted payments. Resignations came in. The total attrition was 205; many who resigned had not been using the club and the financial hit came as the last straw. On the other hand many honorary life members chose to pay the assessment voluntarily. Skee remarked later, "We had to do it quickly because of the bank loan." As Dick Maier, Skee's successor, said, "A lot of the financial pressure was reduced when Skee got that assessment. After that the interest wasn't as onerous. But the most significant thing during my second tenure on the board was the change in membership — we were no longer a richly "have" club. At the time of the assessment there was a lot of unhappiness — four years of attrition compressed into a year and a half. The waiting list turned out to be very soft."

On the bright side, up on the third floor members were getting fit. They were getting fit by the hundreds. Initial tentative approaches to a fitness facility had been, "It will only be used in the winter. It is a passing fad." But by the second year of its operation more than 900 members had been tested for a program, and 400 were using the fitness room on a regular basis, that is 60 to 70 members

Some of the faithful 6:00 a.m. fitness group.
Front row. Janet Wilson, Gord Mollenhauer, Joyce Seagram, Martha Butterfield. Second row. Wendy Rolph, Joann Moysey, Judy Korthals, Ginny Kent. Third row. Tony Rolph, Clayton Scott, John de Pencier, Kathy Martin, Diana Tremain, Sally Forrest Fourth row. George Wilson, Gay Evans, Chris Kelson, Neil Guthrie, Gill Evans.

on the machines each day. Eleanor O'Gorman, from her pro shop in the platform tennis hut, had worked on selecting the fitness equipment. "We had a budget. Mary Knowles was involved as head of the Sports Committee with Dr. Sydney Smart and Jennifer Whelpton on the committee as well. I worked with a consultant and we looked at different facilities. I did lots of networking. It was fun and we came in right on budget." And Eleanor hired Milan Jablonsky.

A mock graduation in the fitness room staged at 6:00 a.m. for Diana Tremain on the day of her real graduation in the B.A. program at the University of Toronto. Left to right Ian Scott, sceptre bearer, John de Pencier, chancellor, Diana with her hand on the chancellor's knee, John Evans greeting the graduates.

Not a passing fad. Ray Smith, Janet Belknap and Keith Townley in the fitness room.

"I was a teacher working for Dawson College, an English college in downtown Montreal. I taught there for eighteen years. Then we moved to Mississauga and I was commuting weekly between Mississauga and Montreal for almost four years. I wanted to find a job in the Toronto area, preferably at the university or college level from which I came. Over the weekends I started to work in the Donalda Club. Then I heard that the B&R was planning to open a fitness club. I had a meeting with Eleanor to talk about it — that was in the summer of 1989. Eleanor said she was looking for someone to take a full-time position, so I took two years leave of absence from Montreal. Then after two years I gave up Montreal.

We started to use the small hut and conducted assessments. Before we even opened we had 450 people. Every half-hour somebody was coming in. A couple of partners and I worked from seven in the morning till seven at night. At the end of December we had five or six pieces of equipment, some top quality, some not. Weights were added to the list and bought. I made different levels of programs. We bunched people together, five or six on the same level. After ten years, we have assessed 2,400 people. We have probably 600 regular users — once a week, some three times a week or more. The increase is remarkable. In

Milan Jablonsky.

Dana Rodziunas.

the winter, which is the peak, there were initially sixty users per day. Now it has doubled to 120. There has been a keen group coming in at 6:00 a.m. and then there was a petition that they should extend the opening. Now we are open at 5:30 a.m.

The trend is growing to have personal trainers — no other trend is stronger. This was approved and now Dana and I do about 60 hours of personal training. A year ago we offered a new trend. We were the first to offer it — personal group training. Sometimes it is like a zoo up here, but it is wonderful. Almost half the active membership of the club uses the fitness centre. And we have not even had a minor accident in ten years. I have probably used three bandages in all that time. Now we even offer massage. John D'Aguanno and I meet to discuss common things. Sometimes John will recommend fitness training to people."

On the tennis front there was a proud moment in 1993 when Gilbert Nunns and Bob Bedard were appointed to the Hall of Fame of Tennis Canada. There was good news on the home front, as well. Two courts would be made available for B&R members at Upper Canada College, weekdays after five and all day Saturday, in the end a much better solution than the Cottingham proposal.

As well, there was another very pressing issue that came to a happy conclusion. At the request of the house committee ladies would now be allowed to wear pantsuits or appropriate dress pants into the main dining room.

Back at the board table the talk was of operating losses, the loss of special functions, reduced dining room and bar use, a small waiting list, more resignations than expected. It was difficult to keep the membership level up to the desired 2,500 whereas the difficulty in 1986 had been to keep a lid on the 2,500 level. And there were ongoing nec-

> "Derek was the pro and I was chair of squash. We had speeches. Derek started the meeting. He said a few words and followed with, 'I'm now turning the meeting over to Peter Hatcher.' As soon as he said that I started to say, 'Ladies and gentlemen.' Billy Hatch, who had organized everyone, along with Maggie, got up, and everyone in the room walked out. When they were all out Hatchy came back and said, 'Are you through yet?'"
> *Peter Hatcher*

> "It was great coming here for lunch on Saturday. There was John Armour, Tony Ormsby, Dick Wise. The senior members would have lunch in the Maple Room and the younger ones, under forty, weren't invited. There might be twenty, thirty men there for lunch. Just before I became president I had the temerity to go into the room and listen."
> *Dick Maier*

> "It's funny the perspective you grow up with. Some people tell me they felt uncomfortable as a junior. I always felt perfectly relaxed and comfortable. I came in with my big black bear shaggy boots in the wintertime and Murphy would poke his head out of the pro shop and would come out with a racquet and start hitting my boots, calling out, 'I'll kill them.' He was a character. We had our junior lounge. We would close the door for a while and then someone would say, 'Let's go out and play.' I tried to get on the competitive badminton team here, called the Pepsi team, and when I didn't make it I got into squash with my sister. We were one of the first girls. Nancy Henderson was active then. We hosted a tournament here and Derek stuck me in, and that's when it happened. I started with hardball but I love softball now. And now my daughters come in and they have buddies here."
> *Sue Behan*

J. Roy Mansell
Tennis

Inducted into the
Tennis Hall of fame
1994

Canadian Senior
Men's Doubles (55+)
1973

Canadian Masters
Men's Indoor Doubles
(70+)
1988

> "Tom McCarthy used to play hard in squash. A discussion started about how well Tom played and how hard he played and that he could probably take Chink 15 — 0. Chink said no way. They made a $500 bet. Chink would have a 12-point advantage. Tom won. The next year they had the same bet. I think Chink got 13. Tom won again. The next year I was chairman of squash. Derek and I got some prizes. We got a T-shirt for Chink with '500' on it. When we gave it to him he took off his jacket and tie and put on his T-shirt and did a dance."
> *Doug Bower*

The Gilbert family: Phil, with Katie and Jayne

essary capital expenses unrelated to the renovations, such as $85,000 for a new badminton floor. Entrance fees did not cover regular needed improvements. A break-even operation does not cover depreciation. In 1991 two possible solutions were put forward. The first was a social membership, rejected because the B&R had always been a playing family club. The second was minimum house accounts. Both were vetoed.

The financial position continued to tax successive boards. David Higginbotham, president in 1993, inherited an operating loss and a major disruption in senior staff. For a time he needed to wear several hats. The departure of Pat McCann, the secretary manager, in the spring of 1993, and food and beverage manager, Leo Chan, left a vacuum.

"David," says Peter Hatcher, "was practically the general manager." Then David Brightling was appointed general manager. He had a degree from the University of Toronto and training in hospitality management from George Brown College, and had worked for eight years at the RCYC, latterly as assistant general manager. Brightling then spent two years in human resources at the Granite Club, and two as general manager at St. George's Golf Club. At the B&R he initiated regular weekly meetings of food and beverage staff and department heads, with day-long training sessions for staff concerning service and wine training. Systems were being put in place.

David Brightling.

> "This was always home away from home for me as a kid. I always felt welcome here. I love the place. Here I can sit at the bar and have a half sandwich and a bowl of soup because I feel it is home. There are so many friends and relatives. This is pretty much when I started dating my husband — at a platform tennis party. As far as the social facilities are concerned there are few of us who can play tennis and then sit around and have lunch. Members are not looking to the club for their social activities. They have only so much time for entertainment."
>
> Wendy Jarvis

But the average member was probably less au courant with the B&R's bank account or staff changes than with the affair of the infamous pool table. Purchased in 1993, it was put in the Maple Room, which was off limits to the female half of the club. This caused no small amount of consternation, as pool was no longer only a man's game. Use of the pool table became a "back-room issue." There were radical possibilities, including allowing women into the Maple Room after 8:00 p.m. There were secret excursions after a party. After advice from the Young Members' Advisory Committee, led by Peter Hatcher, a decision was made. The billiard room would be available for mixed company, informally dressed, after 8:00 p.m. daily except on Tuesday, which was games night. Sue Sisam, a board member, said the new rule was an open invitation to go down for a game of pool after the board meeting. "Nothing could have kept me from the pool table. Even if it was the last thing I felt like doing, on a point of principle I was there with cue in hand."

> "We didn't want to deny juniors the use of the club, but were anxious to keep the numbers in a positive state. We had a large number of juniors paying low fees. We proposed to abolish that category and allow young members the same privileges, but as card-holders. This meant we could bring more seniors in to the club. But the wheel turns and we have junior memberships again now."
> *Bill Heintzman*

In 1994, for the first time in its seventy years, the club had a woman president, Elsie Falconer. It was not an easy time. "My big challenges," she recalls, "were a change of manager and the club just recovering from the renovations and the recession. There was a recession mentality. There were overdue accounts of as much as $3,000. As well, I was the first woman president so I was going to tread very carefully. It started with a bang. At my first meeting there was a membership blow-up to deal with. Then Fran's came up for sale again, so we considered it, but it was not practical. We briefly considered buying the building next door for relatively little cash up front, using the ground floor space for the club and carrying it by renting out all the office space. But it would mean carrying a huge mortgage, and that would not have rested comfortably with the membership." The smoking policy was up for discussion with two

Elsie Falconer, president in 1994, the first woman to fill that post.

A keen badminton player, Philip "Pip" Byers.

Chink Fleming on the Sidelines

"David Bassett, who has won the tennis and the singles squash here and is an outstanding player, was playing with his partner Doug Brown, who is also an outstanding player. I was playing with my partner against them. David is very outspoken. English is his second language. His primary language is profanity. For every shot David would yell 'mine' and 'I've got it.' One shot was hit about five feet away from Doug. David runs back yelling 'mine' and the ball hits him on the head. Chink Fleming, who was watching the match, called out, 'It's lucky you're not curling, David!'"

Terry Corcoran

"Terry Corcoran was playing Heather McKay, [an Australian, and the undisputed number one lady squash player in the world.] Naturally, there was a big gallery. Terry took it very seriously and got into phenomenal shape, playing every day. Chink was standing at the side of the gallery with his drink. In the first rally they must have hit the ball fifty times, and Heather was running Terry around. She won the point and Chink called out, 'Way to run her around Corc!' When Terry was exhausted he missed a point. Chink said, 'Well, you sure have her number.'" [The match was reported in the club's sports letter, in which Terry's sportsmanship was praised, "How many other players of his calibre and personality would have been prepared to be thrown to the lions (or lioness) in front of almost a hundred club members. The only thing he lost was the match.]

Doug Bower

strong factions in disagreement. Dress code was being studied, with most wanting no change. Baby-sitting was new and there was much to discuss — location, fees, how many children could be cared for. The operating losses continued. The debt would not be paid off until 1997.

Out on the courts there was a drop of interest in squash, so Victor Harding undertook a study of that situation and of the club's development program for all ages and stages in racquet sports. "There were some of us," he said, "who felt that the club should make a better effort to recognize excellence in competitive sports and reward it by paying attention to it. This way others are encouraged to excel. Also we should make sure that in each sport there are clinics for junior, intermediate, and senior players. And as part of this whole theory we should be able to identify a talented player at the age of ten, eleven, twelve, and develop that talent. Right now we are a better club, with our active house leagues at different levels and our dedicated pros. We need to continue to pay attention to excellence."

Eleanor agrees. "Victor is right. You have to drive everything from the bottom up. For Paul and me tennis takes most of our dedication. We needed a dedicated pro for badminton. Stephane Cadieux is doing a great job there. In squash Eric Baldwin has increased the participation from one hundred to two or three hundred. Paddle tennis has

Eric Baldwin with Shaine Currie and George Grant.

Stephane Cadieux.

fifty active players. Paul is good there, too. Competition is important. Parents or coaches can't make anyone want to work at a sport. But if someone beats you by one point then you will want to press next time to get that extra point. We have held junior badminton tournaments for the first time since the Wansbrough girls played as juniors. Now Strachan Jarvis, Stephen MacPhail, and Conor Behan, are fairly high up in the Ontario Badminton Association. Squash is the same. We were short of post-university women in squash. We got something started three years ago. Now more women are getting involved in squash."

In 1998 Joanne Morton retired from the B&R. She has the history of the club in her memories, of members and their eccentricities, of renovations, of managers.

"There were lots of original members still around when I started — Mrs. Armstrong, Mrs. Bacque, Mrs. Bell, Mrs. Boone, Mrs. Currelly, Mrs. Fairty, Mrs. Fergusson, Mrs. Gooderham, Mrs. Gouinlock, Mrs. Humphrey, Mrs. Howe, Mrs. Risdon, Mrs Stephenson, Mrs, Suydam, the Warwick sisters, Mrs. Ireton, Mrs. Leishman, Mr. Bacque, Mr. Blackstock, Mr. Dyment, Mr. Flemming, Mr. Ellis, Mr. Harrison, Mr. Howard, Mr. Laidlaw, Mr. Oakley.

"When I came Mr. Jackson was the manager. He was very strict but very fair. He said, 'Can you do this? Can you do that?' 'No,' I said. 'Oh, that's great,' he said, 'then I can show you my way.' Mr. Longmore used to come in at six o'clock in the morning. When he came in one day

Joanne Morton at her retirement party with her husband, Bill, and Diane Hammond. Diane joined the B&R office staff in 1963, worked with Joanne through thick and thin, and retired in 1995.

there was a couple that were locked in the platform tennis hut. They had been in there when the night watchman came along. They hid from him and then he locked the door. You couldn't open the door from inside."

"Chink Fleming knows something about almost everything."

"One member had lost weight and was a good deal thinner. One day when he was out on the courts Diane and I were looking out the window. He went up to serve the ball and his shorts fell off."

B&R players in the Canadian Platform Tennis Open, 1995. Back: John Waldie, Dundee Staunton, Michael Harding, Mark Duffield. Left to right Cathy Fauquier, Bill Lovering, Strachan Bongard. Front Abigail Abouchar, Oker Ross, Jeannie Parker, Brenda Northey, Joy Waldie, Di Mara.

Wendy and Pearce Jarvis, Graeme and Stephanie Jewett.

"When I started at the club you would never see women in slacks. And everything was pure white in the sports. I remember that when it came time to open the membership for applications people would have breakfast in Fran's to be at the door in time. They would do that for the Christmas dance. They would line up at our door and by 10:30 the dance was sold out."

While financial woes were preoccupying successive boards, the club lost a devoted and popular president, Tony Wells. Tony loved the B&R, and it was a proud moment for him when he became president at the annual meeting in December 1994. He was very ill with the cancer he had been fighting, but his words as incoming president were typically upbeat and positive with the inimitable Wells touch.

"The year 1994," he said, "will be remembered as the year of the skillful and sensitive woman; 1995 will be remembered as the year of the marvelous midget. We have had vertically challenged presidents but they did not seek to end the discrimination against the altitudinally disadvantaged, which exists in the current sports rules, particularly in tennis. I am recommending a new set of rules to be known as the B&R Fair Play Rules, which may become famous throughout the world.

A Family Club for the Nineties

A "Perfect," Tony Wells, with referee, Murray Sullivan, and a "Grosser," Chris Wansbrough.

Tennis players will be divided into three groups according to length.

Those under five feet six will be known as the Perfects, because that's what they are. They absorb less animal, vegetable and mineral matter and create less waste. Those who are over five feet eleven are grossly overlength and will be known as the Grossers. Those from five foot six to five foot eleven are in a state of limbo, some still growing or shrinking, and therefore they are in a type of length purgatory, and will be known as the Purgs. The Grossers will continue to serve from the base line but will have only one serve and it will be underhand. The Perfects will serve from the service line and will have two serves unless serving to a Grosser, in which case they can

Every month for many years, Harry Dawson, eighty-nine-year-old Hi-Tech Pro extraordinaire, actively recruited sixteen men and sixteen women to play in the over popular Hi-Tech Round Robin. Harry established the format. A buffet dinner is served from 6:30 to 8:30 for those who want to eat before, during, or after playing. Play begins for half of the players at 7:15, with a five-minute warm-up and fifteen minutes of fierce competition for the highest score. The other players begin at 7:35 and start with a five-minute warm-up and fifteen minutes of play. With all four courts in play for twenty-minute cycles, from 7:15 until 10:15, players have new partners and new opponents, and chalk up points for first and second prizes. A special bonus prize is awarded to two exceptional players for their good sportsmanship. Harry can take pride in the round robin he organized for over ten years, and in which he was an active participant, making sure that the Hi-Tech was complete with thirty-two enthusiastic tennis players.

Reed Ballon and David Stevenson, squash champions.

Excerpts From A Tribute To Tony Wells

And last year at the B&R
When he should have been in bed,
He played three tennis finals
And won three championships instead.

But it is not for games alone,
Nor his super racquet skills,
That Tony was elected
To the position he now fills.

But rather it's his leadership
That causes all to feel
That the B&R's great president
Has such very great appeal.
Edward Ballon, 1995

Another victory for Victor Harding.

> "The sports lounge is a good area — open, bright, and you can watch people. When I was here as a junior we used to sit in the junior lounge or watch the badminton. The courts were empty on the weekends and so we could have a tennis court to ourselves. We would come in the morning and have lunch and stick around and play."
>
> *Sara Adamson*

have as many serves as necessary. A lob hit by a Grosser or a Purg which lands beyond the service line will be automatic loss of point."

After Tony Wells's death David Higginbotham was asked to return for a second term as president. He informed the membership that Tony had been touched by seeing a photograph of the president's board showing his name.

David Higginbotham identified the need to get the membership back to its 1980s level of 2,500, a five percent increase. One hundred new members were needed. There were necessary expenses. The lack of air conditioning in a club that was enjoying more summer use became a problem. The main lounge, upper bar and Blackstock Room needed refurbishing, and the kitchen needed equipment. These upgrades were vital if new members were to be attracted. To rectify these problems would take $850,000. Operating losses had existed for several years. Bar revenue was down.

Solutions were needed. And they were found. Those who had resigned would be offered the chance to come back with no financial penalty. Entrance fees would become more attractive for spouses and couples joining together and for the sixty-five to seventy age bracket. A sports fee would be introduced, the brain wave of Ruth Grant on the membership committee. A change in procedure would bring new members in each month and the club would encourage applications for children, grandchildren, brothers and sisters of current members.

In the next year results began to show as president Peter Hatcher brought all these policies to fruition with the help of a reviving economy. The response to the mem-

> "The badminton improvement is tremendous. The younger ones now are competing well. I feel when I walk in here that I belong. It's a small place. There are people who use this club on their own schedule at specific times — some are regular users early, some mid-afternoon, and some later on. No matter what hour you come in you still see people you know. I have talked to some new members and people who are thinking of joining and they like the smallness. It's not a massive sports complex. They like getting to know a lot of the members."
>
> *Gill Evans*

"The best thing I did in 1986 was to hire Eleanor."
Peter Townley

bership drive was exciting, and Hatcher reported that a predicted operating loss of $50,000 was reduced to $20,000 with a modest surplus predicted for 1997. He summed up the situation: "David Higginbotham identified the issues and defined them. He deserves a ton of credit for identifying them so precisely and defining them so well. It was fortunate or smart that we happened to work together. We had always had this big waiting list, then Ontario had a recession in the late 1980s and a whole layer of middle management disappeared. As computers came in, middle management was squeezed out. Then there was the recession and lots of people didn't feel they could afford the club. With the renovation people were faced with shelling out, and many resigned. When we approached the waiting list the response often was 'I'll think about it.'"

"We had to start doing things that some of the other clubs were doing. People were becoming more family-oriented. We had to make the club more attractive to younger families. The fine line is not giving away too much to get members. As returning director I chaired a Young Members' Advisory Committee to find out what we needed to do to keep a strong and positive section coming along. There were twelve of us, and we met every couple of months. I gave them a direct link to the board and we talked about all the issues that were important to young members. One of the things they pushed the hardest for was to allow their guests to use a credit card, because they couldn't afford to treat them. They wanted a proper baby-sitting facility and junior program initiatives. I was very proud of the Young Members' Advisory Committee and their great contribution. With these changes and our new facility, the B&R was becoming the hottest in place to be."

The membership drive came to fruition in John de Pencier's time. "Now that we had the open door for returning members," he notes, "we had a great response of almost fifty. We had people in their eighties and nineties re-joining to play bridge. One was ninety-three. We had a real turn-around." In 1996 there was a deficit of more than $100,000. That position was better than expected by the time John de Pencier gave his presidential report in 1997. (John had been called away on an emergency trip to England, so, bringing the B&R onto the cutting edge of technology, he delivered his annual report on video. It went well, except one member told John that he swivelled so much in his swivel chair that it made him seasick to watch.) There was an operating surplus of $262,761 due to increased membership, and more sports fees than expected. "And then there was the subject of making the members' lounge co-ed. I had two meetings. At the second one there were about fifty people. It was a 'back-room issue' and took some getting used to, but the times weren't standing still, nor were the lady members." Soon women could be seen tippling in what had been the last male bastion of the B&R.

During John's presidency a survey was taken (1997) to which forty-three percent of the members responded, indicating their general satisfaction with the facilities and administration of the club, but announcing a basic wish list — expansion to tennis and fitness, now the two most popular areas of the B&R, and concern about that perennial subject, the parking problem.

In May, 1998, the club lost one of its most popular members. His sense of humour would be sorely missed. Ramsey Fraser, member for more than 50 years, died at age 87. Over the years he had served in many capacities, and his reports, whatever the subject, were memorable. He could even lighten up a treasurer's report with his quips. His son, John, now Master of Massey College, paid tribute to his father's tennis and sporting spirit in an article in *The Sunday Star* on Father's Day. He wrote about their last game of tennis.

It was only ten years ago. Whatever strength he had lost through encroaching age, he compensated for with some of the sneakiest shots in the game.

I was always hopeless against his deft psychological warfare. If I missed a shot, for example, he always managed to inquire whether there was "trouble at work" in such a way as to ensure I would miss the next two.

If I ever got a little ahead, the countenance on the other side always grew very serious.

He loved winning so much and knew me so well, he could put me off simply by telling me how well — how surprisingly well — I was doing and follow it up with the stinkiest arcing lob in competitive play.

And he always made me laugh about it.

I once ran into David Macdonald, the former Tory cabinet minister, who had a similar father. "There's a special moment in a young man's life when the son takes over physically from the father," Macdonald observed. "It's a rite of passage that usually happens when the son is 16 or 17. Now I'm 49 and you're 41. When do you suppose it will be our turn?"

Ramsey Fraser.

Robin Logie
Squash

Canadian Men's Doubles (65+) 1998

Howie Rober
Squash

Canadian Men's Doubles (65+) 1998

World Men's Doubles (65+) 1998

In my case, as it happened, never.

On the day I figured the Fates had chosen for me to beat my father, he seemed very old. He had tension bandages around one knee and two elbows. The circulation in his right leg was sluggish. The pacemaker was ticking away. The eyesight was dimming. It wasn't going to be a great victory, but — dammit! — a win's a win.

The first set was mine at seven-five and I was leading three-zip in the second when I made the blunder of a lifetime.

"I'm going to write a column about finally beating you," I told him as we changed service sides.

What a fool!

This was all he needed to spur him on to his last hurrah. He took back the second set six-three and left the court two games up in the third. In a final flourish, he even managed an insidious shot that had the ball hitting the rim of the net, rolling a few inches sideways and then plopping down on my side. I never got near it.

"That's enough," he said with a smile, "I'm retiring from singles on that shot."

The year before the seventy-fifth anniversary the president, John Richardson, was able to report that membership had reached the 2,750 mark, with record use of fitness, and with more than $100,000 in new equipment, good activity in tennis, and increased use of social facilities. The Trophy Room, summer bistro, and bridge areas were bustling, and sports fee registration was strong. There were plans to continually upgrade the facilities with up to $500,000 per year in a five-year maintenance and capital expenditure plan. This followed initiatives from the 1997 membership survey which stressed the need to make the club 'family friendly."

It was left for Don Moffatt to preside over the seventy-fifth anniversary celebrations orchestrated by Bill Munro

Bruce Harrison presenting the Harrison trophy for Over 70 to rivals Joe Nixon, Meredith Fleming, Murray Young, Bob Grant.

and his committee. There was a Canadian Doubles Squash championship, a nostalgic tea dance, a tennis extravaganza featuring teams of members representing the decades, followed by a dance, a B&R junior classic badminton tournament, a casual dinner dance featuring The Saturday Night Fish Frye Band and the singing of our own Carol Welsman, a Canadian mixed platform tennis championship, and finally a very special and memorable Christmas dance."

Seventy-five years had brought physical and social changes to the club as it tried to follow life-styles in a volatile environment. Three major reconstruction periods, 1949, 1964 and, the most dramatic, 1989, had created a facility that responded to the needs of its members. In the final stage, the popular sports lounge had brought many members out of the back rooms of the club leaving that section ready for renewed use. Now the floor of one of the 1924 singles squash courts is visible in the Maple Room. At age seventy-five the B&R is alive and well, and the old car barns are en route to one hundred years of vigour and fun.

A group of long term staff, ranging from twenty-five years to forty-five years with the club, and some more recent employees, gathered to reminisce. Their comments are not attributed, but some serve to turn the mirror back upon the members in jocular spirit.

"The night watchman locked the doors, and checked the windows. Then he heard singing. It was about two o'clock in the morning. A man and women were in the men's showers."

"Murphy and I used to cover the front door. That was before the renovations. We used to do that shift till eleven o'clock when the club closed. There was a party here one time. Murph was on the phone at the main desk. I called in and, in a kid's voice said, 'Is my mommy there?' He said, 'Who are you?' in that big gruff voice. I gave him a name. He had to go all the way upstairs looking for my mommy."

"Once the police chased a man in here who had a gun. They chased him along St. Clair. He ran down the parking lot and into the club. We saw him run right into the ladies locker room. He didn't know which way he was going."

Staff of more than twenty years.
John and Maria, Manfred and Lopes.

"There was one member, who, when coming to the club for his Sunday morning tennis game, sometimes found our parking lot was full, so he would go over to Miles Funeral Home, across the road, and park in their lot. Then he would get out of his car with his bathrobe on and, in bare feet, come across St. Clair and go to his locker."

"On Saturday we would set up the big table more than once. Oh, what they drank! One Saturday I was working. Bob was always the bartender. We served the table. When the lunch was over they got drinking stingers — white crème de menthe and brandy. I ran out of brandy. I used rye instead — the crème de menthe would kill the taste. They didn't notice."

John, Lopes, and Jimmy.

"We were putting up the Christmas decorations for the dance and the ladies were telling us exactly where each thing looked best. I got up on the ladder and held one up and then the ladies would say 'A bit to the left, no, a bit up and to the right.' When they weren't looking I put it back where it had been in the beginning and they said that was perfect."

"There were a lot of players who thought they were better than they really were."

After an afternoon of meetings, the new manager, David Brightling, called the front desk to get messages. "Murphy, this is David Brightling. Are there any messages for me?" "Who?" came back the reply. "I've never heard of you." Click. Dial Tone. Undaunted, the manager tried again. The reception was the same. "Look," said Murphy, "I don't know you. Stop bugging me." Click. Dial tone. Hoping that third time was lucky David tried again. "Now listen carefully Murphy. You know who I am." "No I don't." was the stubborn reply. "Murphy, think boss, as in your new boss." Short silence. "Oh Shit!" Thereafter David always got his messages, but they were usually marked David Who?

One day a club employee was leaving his bank on the corner of St. Clair and Yonge when he heard his name being called. Looking across the street he saw an elderly B&R lady member. She ran across the street to greet him, and exclaimed, "I'm so excited. I just got my new teeth." Whereupon, to make sure he appreciated this piece of news, she took out her new dentures and showed them to him as well as to some other interested pedestrians who happened to be on the spot. The employee politely admired them, saying whatever was appropriate when viewing new teeth.

Remembering the Time — The 75th Anniversary

The Past Directors' Dinner, 1999.

First Row: Donald Moffat, Peter Townley, Bob Grant, John Richardson, John de Pencier, Bev Westcott, Elsie Falconer, Ernie Howard, Bill Munro, Peter Hatcher, Jock Maynard, Ian Stewart. **Second Row:** Alan Watson, Cathy Fauquier, Annabelle Heintzman, Graeme Jewett, Doug Lawson, Pat Davidson, Paul Bolte, Aug Bolte, Anne Nichols, Phil MacDonnell, Jennifer Whelpton, Peter Barnard, David Higginbotham, George Currie, Doug Haldenby. **Third Row:** George Welsman, Bob Cameron, D'Arcy Doherty, Jim McMyn, Sue Sisam, Robin Logie, Alastair Gillespie, Joan Randall, Phil Gilbert, Nancy Ross, Kathy Crossgrove, Peter Gooderham. **Fourth Row:** Maggie Corcoran, Bill Heintzman, Doug Grant, John Yarnell, John Clappison, Ann Kerwin, Jack Mollenhauer, Wendy Jarvis, Doug Bower, Gill Evans, Warren Moysey, Jim Cairncross. **Fifth Row:** Richard Seagram, Don Crawford, Bill Minton, David Gossage, St. Clair Balfour, Bob Bertram, David Kent, Pat Northey, Strachan Heighington, Bill Berghuis, John Fleming.

Pat and Bill Munro, Marie Dalton at the dinner on the tennis weekend.

Team members, in performance. Cathy Fauquier, Bill Munro, Heather Irwin, Bev Bowen, Cathie Hyland, Phil Gilbert.

Recovering from the tennis extravaganza. Susan Townley, Hugh Judges, Florence Salmond, President, 1999, Don Moffat, Peter Salmond, Anne Churchill-Smith, organizer.

Enthusiastic participant, tennis weekend.

Jock Maynard ready for action.

Tea Dance Conveners Maggie Corcoran, Annabelle Heintzman, Nonnie Jennings.

The weekend of Canadian doubles squash at the B&R. Judy Hatcher with squash competitors Howie Rober and Robin Logie.

The anniversary tea dance. Grant Brown, Elizabeth Bell, Barbara Cooper, Katherine (Blackstock) Brown, Colonel Blackstock's daughter.

Revellers in period costume at the anniversary tea dance.
Left to right: Larry Heisey, R-J. Gilbert,
Humphrey Gilbert, Ann Heisey.

The Christmas dance, 1999.

The staff Christmas party, 1999.

The Club Today — The Games Our Members Play

Juniors feeling at home. Among them are:
Ryan Butler, Nicholas Townley, Geordie Fleming, Conor Behan.

Gord Currie, Duncan McGregor, Doug Sanderson.

Bob Langmuir, Murray Young, Bob Grant, Lorne Laing.

The Club Today — The Games Our Members Play

Maureen Hunter, Signy Farncomb, Heather Irwin,
Rosemary Morton, Cate Woodward, Susan Gouinlock.

Nancy Hately, Merrilyn Driscoll,
Win Barclay, Denny Starritt.

Andrea Essen, Neil Ashby,
Sue and Michael Crossley.

Betty Cassels, Barbara MacNaughtan, Joyce Woyen, Denyse
O'Donoghue, Barbara Langfeldt.

Gordon Chiu, Quang Hoang.

If you can't remember the score.

Appendix

Club Presidents 1924-2000

Lt. Col. G. G. Blackstock	1924-1927	J. G. Crean	1949
G. R. Larkin	1928-1929	P. B. Greey	1950
H.N. Baird	1930	H. W. Weis	1951
Dr. E. M. Henderson	1931	F. G. Rolph	1952
G. T. Pepall	1932-1933	C. M. King	1953
Norman Seagram	1934	J. M. Taylor	1954
J. W. Ritch	1935	E. V. Rechnitzer	1955
J. C. Suydam	1935	R. C. Scrivener	1956
P. J. Hanley	1936	J. R. Fraser	1957
H. R. Douglas	1937	A. J. R. May	1958
R. B. Duggan	1938	J. S. Proctor	1959
G. R. Medland	1939	G. H. Craig	1960
J. Graeme Watson	1940	J. E. Kennedy	1961
J. H. Scandrett	1941	T. D. Boynton	1962
F. H. Bacque	1942	P. K. Hanley	1963
J. K. McCausland	1942	R. B. Somerville	1964
T. Oakley	1943	R. W. Finlayson	1965
H. H. Lawson	1944	R. I. Hendy	1966
G. B. Strathy	1945	J. C. Maynard	1967
E. E. Ryerson	1946	D. R. Musgrave	1968
R. S. Morris	1947	L. J. H. Gunn	1969
R. F. Wilson	1948	Ernest Howard	1970

D. S. Mills	1971
B. B. Westcott	1972
R. D. Grant	1973
W. M. Hatch	1974
R. D. Jennings	1975
Ian C. Stewart	1976
P. M. Stewart	1977
W. J. Corcoran	1978
J. E. Foy	1979
W. D. Heintzman	1980
P. G. Townley	1981
W. G. Munro	1982
D. B. Redfern	1983
J. C. C. Wansbrough	1984
A. G. Watson	1985
P. G. Townley	1986
P. R. Barnard	1987
W. G. Munro	1988
D. C. Haldenby	1989
J. A. McClelland	1990
R. M. Maier	1991
G. N. M. Currie	1992
D. C. Higginbotham	1993
Mrs. Elsie Falconer	1994
A. C. B. Wells	1995
D. C. Higginbotham	1995
P. B. Hatcher	1996
J. D. de Pencier	1997
J. E. Richardson	1998
D. O. Moffat	1999
A. W. Moysey	2000

Chairmen of Ladies' Committee

1946	Mrs. W.L. Lovering
1947	Mrs. A.M. Garden
1948	Mrs. Douglas Ham
1949J	Mrs. Douglas Ham
1950J	Mrs. J.P. McRae
1951	Mrs. G. Nunns
1952	Mrs. J.P. McRae
1953	Mrs. J.H. Chipman
1954	Mrs. J.H. Chipman
1955	Mrs. W.Y. Pinkerton
1956	Mrs. Dennison Denny
1957	Mrs. K.W. Peacock
1958	Mrs. F. Des Tombe
1959	Mrs. A.C. Proctor
1960	Mrs. M.K. Pendleton
1961	Mrs. M.K. Pendleton
1962	Mrs. D.G. Guest
1963	Mrs. W.L. McDonald
1964	Mrs. Bruce West

1965 Mrs. J.A. McClelland
1966 Mrs. B.P. Hunter
1967 Mrs. C.D. Suydam
1968 Mrs. O.B. Mabee
1969 Mrs. W.P. Wilder
1970 Mrs. G.H. Heintzman
1971 Mrs. D.J. Eastmure
1972 Mrs. R.K. Martin
1973 Mrs. C.P. Stow
1974 Mrs. D. Guest
1975 Mrs. R.D. Telfer
1976 Mrs. J.M. Godfrey
1977 Mrs. P.M. Stewart
1978 Mrs. R.T. Corcoran
1979 Mrs. W.F. Hood
1980 Mrs. S. Heighington
1981 Mrs. H.M. Cooper
1982 Mrs. J.B. McLeod

List of Canadian and International Champions

Dorothy L. Boone
Badminton
    Canadian Open Ladies Singles 1922
    Canadian Ladies Doubles 1922, 1923, 1924, 1925, 1926, 1928

Esme F. Coke
Badminton
    Canadian Ladies Singles 1924, 1925, 1926, 1928, 1929
    Canadian Ladies Doubles 1924, 1925, 1926, 1928
    Canadian Mixed Doubles 1925

Mrs. Ruggles George
Badminton
    Canadian Ladies' Doubles 1922, 1923

Cyril K. F. Andrewes
Tennis
    Member Canadian Davis Cup Team 1924

Badminton
    Canadian Men's Doubles 1928, 1930, 1931

John de N Kennedy
Badminton
    Canadian Mixed Doubles 1925

John S. Proctor
Tennis
    Canadian Open Men's Doubles 1926
    Canadian Mixed Doubles 1925, 1930

John H. Chipman
Squash
    Canadian Men's Amateur Singles 1926

Arthur W. Ham
Tennis
    Member Canadian Davis Cup Team 1926, 1927, 1928, 1929

Gilbert Nunns
Tennis
    Member of the Canadian Davis Cup Team 1927, 1928, 1930, 1931, 1932, 1933, 1934
    Canadian Open Men's Doubles 1937
    Canadian Junior Men's Singles 1924, 1925
    Inducted into the Canadian Tennis Hall of Fame 1993

George G. Blackstock
Badminton
    Canadian Men's Doubles 1928, 1930, 1931

John M. Taylor
Badminton
    Canadian Men's Singles 1931

Walter M. Martin
Tennis
    Member Canadian Davis Cup Team 1931, 1932, 1933, 1934
    Canadian Open Men's Doubles 1937

Hope H. Salmond
Tennis
    Canadian Open Ladies Doubles 1932

John K. McCausland
Squash
    Canadian Men's Doubles 1934

Derek R. Bocquet
Tennis
    British Junior Men's Indoor Singles 1936
    British Junior Men's Indoor Doubles 1936
    British Men's Professional Singles 1951
    British Men's Professional Doubles 1951

Ruby Fisher
Tennis
    Canadian Open Ladies Doubles 1938, 1948

David C. Higginbotham
Squash
    Canadian Junior Men's Singles 1948

Daphne Walker
Badminton
    Canadian Junior Ladies Singles 1951

Harry E. "Budd" Porter
Badminton
    Canadian Men's Doubles 1952, 1953, 1957, 1958
    Canadian Mixed Doubles 1952
    Member Canadian Thomas Cup Team 1952, 1955

Ernest Howard
Squash
    U.S. Men's Singles 1953
    Canadian Men's Singles 1953

Tom D. Boynton
Squash
> Canadian Men's Doubles 1953

Robert P. Bedard
Tennis
> Member Canadian Davis Cup Team 1953, 1955, 1956, 1957, 1958, 1959, 1960, 1961, 1967
> Canadian Open Men's Singles 1955, 1957, 1958
> Canadian Open Men's Doubles 1955, 1957, 1959
> Canadian Closed Men's Doubles 1970
> Member Canadian Pan American Games Team – Silver Medal 1959
> Member Canadian Stevens Cup Team 1985
> Inducted into the Tennis Hall of Fame 1992

Philip A. Greey
Squash
> Canadian Junior Men's Singles 1954

Peter R. Barnard
Tennis
> Canadian Open Junior Men's Doubles 1955
> Canadian Closed Junior Men's Doubles 1955

Beverley B. Westcott
Badminton
> Canadian Men's Doubles 1956
> Member Canadian Thomas Cup Team 1955, 1958, 1961

John F. Bassett
Tennis
> Member Canadian Davis Cup Team 1959
> Canadian Open Junior Men's Doubles 1955
> Canadian Closed Junior Men's Doubles 1955

David E. Bassett
Squash
> Canadian Junior Men's Singles 1960

Don E. Leggat
Squash
> Canadian Men's Singles 1961
> Canadian Men's Veterans Doubles (40+) 1970, 1972, 1975, 1976
> Canadian Men's Doubles (50+) 1981, 1983, 1986
> Canadian Men's Veterans Singles Hardball (40+) 1970, 1973, 1974
> Canadian Men's Singles Hardball (55+) 1984, 1987
> U.S. Men's Veterans Doubles (40+) 1971, 1974, 1975, 1976
> U.S. Men's Senior Doubles (50+) 1981, 1983, 1984, 1985, 1986
> Canadian Men's Singles Hardball (60+) 1993
> World Masters Men's Doubles (50+) 1986
> World Men's Doubles (60+) 1994

Harry E. Fauquier
Tennis
> Member Canadian Davis Cup Team 1962, 1963, 1965, 1966, 1968, 1969, 1971 Captain 1972, 1973
> Canadian Open Junior Men's Doubles 1959

Canadian Open Junior Men's Singles 1959
Canadian Closed Junior Men's Singles 1960
Canadian Open Men's Doubles 1968
Canadian Senior Men's Doubles (45+) 1987, 1989, 1991, 1992

Brenda Nunns
Tennis
Canadian Junior Doubles 1962
Canadian Open Ladies Doubles 1965

Nancy E. Doherty
Tennis
Canadian Junior Ladies Doubles 1965, 1966
Canadian Junior Mixed Doubles 1965, 1966
Canadian Senior Ladies Doubles (35+) 1988
Canadian Senior Ladies Doubles (40+) 1988
Canadian Senior Ladies Indoor Doubles 1988

Platform Tennis
Canadian Ladies Doubles 1981, 1982, 1983, 1985, 1987, 1988, 1989, 1991, 1992

Wally E. Halder
Tennis
Canadian Open Senior Men's Doubles (45+) 1968

Peter B. Hatcher
Platform Tennis
Canadian Men's Doubles 1974, 1983, 1985

Squash
Canadian Men's Doubles (50+) 1992, 1993
Canadian Men's Veteran Singles Hardball (40+) 1986
Canadian Men's Singles Hardball (45+) 1990, 1991
Canadian Men's Singles Hardball (50+) 1992, 1993

J. Martin Walker
Platform Tennis
Canadian Men's Doubles 1974, 1975

Mary Gordon
Platform Tennis
Canadian Ladies Doubles 1976

Ruth Grant
Platform Tennis
Canadian Mixed Doubles 1976
Canadian Ladies Doubles 1976

Doug Grant
Platform Tennis
Canadian Mixed Doubles 1976

Greg R. Halder
Tennis
Member Canadian Davis Cup Team 1977, 1979
Canadian Closed Men's Doubles 1980
Canadian Closed Men's Singles 1980

Susan C. Behan
Squash
    Judy Traviss North American Open Singles 1978

C. M. Victor Harding
Squash
    Canadian Men's Doubles 1978, 1981, 1987
    U.S. Men's Doubles 1977, 1981, 1983
    Canadian Mixed Doubles 1982, 1983, 1984, 1985, 1987. 1988
    U.S. Mixed Doubles 1989
    Canadian Men's Veterans Doubles (40+) 1991, 1992
    World Masters Men's Doubles 1985
    World Veterans Doubles (40+) 1994
    Member Canadian Men's ISRF Team 1977
    Canadian Mixed Veteran Doubles 1995, 1999
    U.S. Veteran Doubles (40+) 1999

Pamela H. O'Rorke
Platform Tennis
    Canadian Ladies Doubles 1981, 1982, 1983, 1984

Charles F. Baird
Platform Tennis
    Canadian Men's Doubles 1981, 1982, 1983, 1984

Tennis
    Canadian Masters Doubles (60+) 1985, 1986

Norma Baird
Platform Tennis
    Canadian Ladies Doubles 1983, 1987

Frank C. Dimock
Tennis
    Canadian Men's Masters Doubles (60+) 1985

John S. Boynton
Squash
    Canadian Mixed Doubles 1986
    Canadian Men's Veterans Doubles (40+) 1990, 1993
    Canadian Men's Doubles 1997, 1998

J. Roy Mansell
Tennis
    Inducted into the Tennis Hall of fame 1994
    Canadian Senior Men's Doubles (55+) 1973
    Canadian Masters Men's Indoor Doubles (70+) 1988

Robin Logie
Squash
    Canadian Men's Doubles (65+) 1998

Howie Rober
Squash
    Canadian Men's Doubles (65+) 1998
    World Men's Doubles (65+) 1998

Club Champions
Badminton
Ladies A Singles
C. Esme Coke Trophy Presemted in 1955

Year	Winners	Year	Winners
1925-26	Mrs. E.F. Coke	1946-47	Mrs. G.J.W. Proctor
1926-27	Mrs. C.A. Boone	1947-48	Pam McPherson
1927-28	Mrs. E.F. Coke	1948-49	Pam McPherson
1928-29	Mrs. E.F. Coke	1949-50	Daphne Walker
1929-30	Mrs. E.F. Coke	1950-51	Daphne Walker
1930-31	Miss M. Lamb	1951-52	Daphne Walker
1931-32	Miss K. Grant	1952-53	Daphne Walker
1932-33	Mrs. E.F. Coke	1953-54	Daphne Walker
1933-34	Mrs. E.F. Coke	1954-55	Daphne Walker
1934-35	Mrs. E.F. Coke	1955-56	Miss A. Greey
1935-36	Mrs. E.F. Coke	1956-57	Mrs. A.G. Richmond
1936-37	Miss M. Lamb	1957-58	Mrs. B. Westcott
1937-38	Mrs. B.B. Geale	1958-59	Mrs. B. Westcott
1938-39	Miss M. Lamb	1959-60	Miss K. Rechnitzer
1939-40	Miss G. Dack	1960-61	Mrs. A.G. Richmond
1940-41	Miss G. Dack	1961-62	Mrs. A.G. Richmond
1941-42	No contest	1962-63	Mrs. B. Westcott
1942-43	No contest	1963-64	Miss K. Rechnitzer
1943-44	No contest	1964-65	Miss K. Rechnitzer
1944-45	No contest	1965-66	Miss K. Rechnitzer
1945-46	Pam McPherson	1966-67	Miss K. Rechnitzer

Year	Winner	Year	Winner
1967-68	Miss K. Rechnitzer	1983-84	Susan Wansbrough
1968-69	Mrs. A.G. Richmond	1984-85	Jane Wansbrough
1969-70	Mrs. D. Eastmure	1985-86	Jane Wansbrough
1970-71	Miss S. Bolte	1986-87	Jane Wansbrough
1971-72	Miss S. Bolte	1987-88	Ruth Wansbrough
1972-73	Miss M. Watt	1988-89	Jane Philp
1973-74	Miss S. Wansbrough	1989-90	Jane Philp
1974-75	Miss S. Wansbrough	1990-91	Sue Crossley
1975-76	Miss S. Wansbrough	1991-92	Sue Crossley
1976-77	Jane Wansbrough	1992-93	Sue Crossley
1977-78	Pam Davidson	1993-94	Sue Crossley
1978-79	Susan Wansbrough	1994-95	Jane Philp
1979-80	Susan Wansbrough	1995-96	Jane Philp
1980-81	Susan Wansbrough	1996-97	no contest
1981-82	No contest	1997-98	Ann Batten
1982-83	Susan Wansbrough	1998-99	Edith Chow

Badminton

Ladies A Doubles

Mrs. F. D. Lace Trophy Presented in 1958

Year	Winners	Year	Winners
1925-26	Mrs. E.F. Coke & Mrs. C.A. Boone	1946-47	Mrs. E.F. Coke & Mrs. C. Owens
1926-27	Mrs. C.A. Boone & Mrs. R. George	1947-48	Mrs. E.F. Coke & Mrs. G. Nunns
1927-28	Mrs. E.F. Coke & Mrs. C.A. Boone	1948-49	Cherith Coke & Pam McPherson
1928-29	Mrs. E.F. Coke & Mrs. C.A. Boone	1949-50	Mrs. B. Westcott & Miss Daphne Walker
1929-30	Mrs. E.F. Coke & Mrs. C.A. Boone	1950-51	Mrs. E.F. Coke & Mrs. H.B. Bowen
1930-31	Miss M. Lamb & Miss M. Ogilvie	1951-52	Mrs. B. Westcott & Miss Daphne Walker
1931-32	Mrs. C.A. Boone & Miss M. Elmsley	1952-53	Miss A. Greey & Miss E. Jackson
1932-33	Mrs. E.F. Coke & Miss M. Lamb	1953-54	Mrs. B. Westcott & Miss B. Bell
1933-34	Mrs. E.F. Coke & Mrs. C.A. Boone	1954-55	Miss Daphne Walker & Miss A. Greey
1934-35	Mrs. E.F. Coke & Mrs. C.A. Boone	1955-56	Mrs. B. Westcott & Miss R. Bell
1935-36	Mrs. E.F. Coke & Mrs. C.A. Boone	1956-57	Mrs. B. Westcott & Mrs. A.G. Richmond
1936-37	Mrs. E.F. Coke & Mrs. C.A. Boone	1957-58	Mrs. B. Westcott & Mrs. R.W. Nicholls
1937-38	Mrs. E.F. Coke & Miss M. Lamb	1958-59	Mrs. B. Westcott & Mrs. R. Nicholls
1938-39	Mrs. E.F. Coke & Miss M. Lamb	1959-60	Mrs. D.N. Greey & Mrs. A.G. Richmond
1939-40	Mrs. E.F. Coke & Miss M. Lamb	1960-61	Mrs. H.M. Cooper & Mrs. A.G. Richmond
1940-41	Mrs. E.F. Coke & Mrs. G. Dack	1961-62	Mrs. D.N. Greey & Mrs. A.G. Richmond
1941-42	No Contest	1962-63	Mrs. G. Nunns & Miss K. Nunns
1942-43	No Contest	1963-64	Mrs. C. Nicholls & Miss K. Rechnitzer
1943-44	No Contest	1964-65	Mrs. D. Eastmure & Mrs. J.L. Mills
1944-45	No Contest	1965-66	Mrs. H.M. Cooper & Mrs. D. Eastmure
1945-46	Mrs. E.F. Coke & Mrs. G.J.W. Proctor	1966-67	Miss K.P. Rechnitzer & Miss E.L. Martin

Year	Winners	Year	Winners
1967-68	Miss K.P. Rechnitzer & Miss L.V. Martin	1983-84	Jane Wansbrough & Susan Wansbrough
1968-69	Mrs. A. Richmond & Mrs. H.M. Cooper	1984-85	Sue Crossley & Jane Wansbrough
1969-70	Mrs. H.M. Cooper & Mrs. D. Eastmure	1985-86	Jane Wansbrough & Ruth Wansbrough
1970-71	Mrs. D. Eastmure & Mrs. B. Westcott	1986-87	Jane Wansbrough & Ruth Wansbrough
1971-72	Mrs. D. Eastmure & Mrs. B. Westcott	1987-88	Ann McPherson & Marian McPherson
1972-73	Mrs. M. Greey & Mrs. A.G. Richmond	1988-89	Jane Philp & Ruth Wansbrough
1973-74	Mrs. D. Eastmure & Mrs. B. Westcott	1989-90	Jane Philp & Ruth Wansbrough
1974-75	Miss M. Watt & Miss S. Wansbrough	1990-91	Jane Philp & Ruth Wansbrough
1975-76	Jane Wansbrough & Susan Wansbrough	1991-92	Sue Crossley & Jane Philp
1976-77	Ann Richmond & Pam Westcott	1992-93	Sue Crossley & Jane Philp
1977-78	Ann Richmond & Pam Westcott	1993-94	Sue Crossley & Jane Philp
1978-79	Jane Wansbrough & Susan Wansbrough	1994-95	Sue Crossley & Jane Philp
1979-80	Susan Wansbrough & Michelle Watt	1995-96	Sara McPherson & Ann Batten
1980-81	Brenda Davidson & Pam Davidson	1996-97	No Contest
1981-82	Brenda Davidson & Pam Davidson	1997-98	Sara McPherson & Ann Batten
1982-83	Jane Wansbrough & Susan Wansbrough	1998-99	Edith Chow & Jennifer Lam

Badminton
Men's A Singles
George C. Blackstock Trophy Presented in 1948-49

Year	Winner	Year	Winner
1925-26	G.G. Blackstock	1946-47	B. Westcott
1926-27	J. de N. Kennedy	1947-48	A. Findlay
1927-28	G.G. Blackstock	1948-49	B. Westcott
1928-29	J.M. Taylor	1949-50	B. Westcott
1929-30	J.M. Taylor	1950-51	B. Westcott
1930-31	J.M. Taylor	1951-52	B. Westcott
1931-32	J.M. Taylor	1952-53	B. Westcott
1932-33	H.A. Henderson	1953-54	B. Westcott
1933-34	H.A. Henderson	1954-55	B. Westcott
1934-35	H.A. Henderson	1955-56	P. Boswell
1935-36	H.A. Henderson	1956-57	B. Westcott
1936-37	H.A. Henderson	1957-58	J. Pinkham
1937-38	W.T. Pinkerton	1958-59	P. Boswell
1938-39	W.T. Pinkerton	1959-60	B. Westcott
1939-40	W.T. Pinkerton	1960-61	J. Pinkham
1940-41	W.T. Pinkerton	1961-62	B. Westcott
1941-42	no contest	1962-63	B. Westcott
1942-43	no contest	1963-64	J. Pinkham
1943-44	no contest	1964-65	J. Pinkham
1944-45	no contest	1965-66	J. Pinkham
1945-46	B. Westcott	1966-67	A. Pequegnat

Year	Winner	Year	Winner
1967-68	A. Pequegnat	1983-84	John Pinkham
1968-69	J. Pinkham	1984-85	Bev Westcott
1969-70	B. Westcott	1985-86	Bev Westcott
1970-71	B. Westcott	1986-87	Richard Thompson
1971-72	J. Pinkham	1987-88	Stephen Hunter
1972-73	D. Johnston	1988-89	Stephen Hunter
1973-74	D. Johnston	1989-90	Stephen Hunter
1974-75	G. Mills	1990-91	Stephen Hunter
1975-76	J. Pinkham	1991-92	Stephen Hunter
1976-77	Geoff Mills	1992-93	Stephen Hunter
1977-78	John Pinkham	1993-94	Stephen Hunter
1978-79	Geoff Mills	1994-95	Stephen Hunter
1979-80	Geoff Mills	1995-96	Stephen Hunter
1980-81	Geoff Mills	1996-97	Stephen Hunter
1981-82	Geoff Mills	1997-98	Stephen Hunter
1982-83	John Pinkham	1998-99	Quang Hoang

David Gossage, Doug Grant, Tony Wells, Chris Ondaatje, Bev Westcott, Terry Wardrop.

Badminton
Men's A Doubles
Lesslie Wilson Trophy Presented in 1978

Year	Winnerss	Year	Winners
1925-26	G.G Blackstock, J de N. Kennedy	1946-47	T.P. Lownsbrough, B. Westcott
1926-27	J. de N. Kennedy, C.K.F. Andrews	1947-48	H.C. Bowen, B.B. Geale
1927-28	G.G Blackstock, J de N. Kennedy	1948-49	A.Y. Eaton, B. Westcott
1928-29	G.G Blackstock, J de N. Kennedy	1949-50	A.Y. Eaton, B. Westcott
1929-30	G.G Blackstock, J de N. Kennedy	1950-51	A.Y. Eaton, B. Westcott
1930-31	G.G Blackstock, J de N. Kennedy	1951-52	A.Y. Eaton, B. Westcott
1931-32	J. M. Taylor, A.E. Snell	1952-53	I. More, B. Westcott
1932-33	C.K.F. Andrewes, H.A. Henderson	1953-54	B. Westcott, J. Moses
1933-34	G.G. Blackstock, H.A. Henderson	1954-55	B. Westcott, A.C.B. Wells
1934-35	J.M. Taylor, C.O. Wood	1955-56	P. Boswell, K. Meredith
1935-36	P.J. Hanley, G.S.H. Cook	1956-57	J. Pinkham, B. Westcott
1936-37	C.K.F. Andrewes, H.A. Henderson	1957-58	K. Meredith, J.A. Pequegnat
1937-38	T.H. Smith, T.P. Lownsbrough	1958-59	K. Meredith, J.A. Pequegnat
1938-39	B. Higgins, T.P. Lownsbrough	1959-60	J.B. McLeod, J. Pinkham
1939-40	B. Higgins, T.P. Lownsbrough	1960-61	H.E. Porter, F.M. Young
1940-41	B.B. Geale, W.T. Pinkerton	1961-62	H.E. Porter, F.M. Young
1941-42	No Contest	1962-63	J.A. Pequegnat, J. Pinkham
1942-43	No Contest	1963-64	J.A. Pequegnat, J. Pinkham
1943-44	No Contest	1964-65	J.A. Pequegnat, J. Pinkham
1944-45	No Contest	1965-66	J. Pinkham, F.M. Young
1945-46	T.P. Lownsbrough, B.B. Geale	1966-67	H.E. Porter, J.E.M. Rolph

Year	Winners	Year	Winners
1967-68	J.A. Pequegnat, J. More	1983-84	Budd Porter & Bev Westcott
1968-69	J. Pinkham, D. Churchill-Smith	1984-85	BuddPorter & Bev Westcott
1969-70	B.B. Westcott, H.E. Porter	1985-86	Budd Porter & Bev Westcott
1970-71	J. A. Pequegnat, H.E. Porter	1986-87	Budd Porter & Bev Westcott
1971-72	J.A. Pequegnat, H.E. Porter	1987-88	Adam dePencier & Stephen Hunter
1972-73	B.B. Westcott, D. Johnston	1988-89	Adam dePencier & Stephen Hunter
1973-74	B.B. Westcott, H.E. Porter	1989-90	Adam dePencier & Stephen Hunter
1974-75	B.B. Westcott, H.E. Porter	1990-91	Adam dePencier & Stephen Hunter
1975-76	Budd Porter & Bev Westcott	1991-92	Adam dePencier & Stephen Hunter
1976-77	Budd Porter & Bev Westcott	1992-93	Stephen Hunter & Sandy Logie
1977-78	Budd Porter & Bev Westcott	1993-94	Stephen Hunter & Sandy Logie
1978-79	Peter Baumann & Geoff Mills	1994-95	Geoff Mills & Bruce Taylor
1979-80	Peter Baumann & Geoff Mills	1995-96	Geoff Mills & Bruce Taylor
1980-81	Budd Porter & Bev Westcott	1996-97	Geoff Mills & Bruce Taylor
1981-82	Budd Porter & Bev Westcott	1997-98	Geoff Mills & Bruce Taylor
1982-83	Mike Moore & Mike Stephenson	1998-99	Quang Hoang & Hollam Sutander

Badminton
Mixed A Doubles
C.W. Beatty Trophy

Year	Winners	Year	Winners
1925-26	Mrs. E.F. Coke, G.G. Blackstock	1946-47	Mrs. E.F. Coke, F.W. Torrance
1926-27	Mrs. C.A. Boone, R.S. Northcote	1947-48	Mrs. G. Nunns, H.C. Bowen
1927-28	Mrs. C.A. Boone, C.K.F. Andrewes	1948-49	Pam McPherson, B. Westcott
1928-29	Mrs. E.F. Coke, C.K.F. Andrewes	1949-50	Mrs. B. Westcott, B. Westcott
1929-30	Mrs. E.F. Coke, C.K.F. Andrewes	1950-51	Mrs. B. Westcott, B. Westcott
1930-31	Mrs. L. Gooderham, J.M. Taylor	1951-52	Mrs. B. Westcott, B. Westcott
1931-32	Mrs. L. Gooderham, J.M. Taylor	1952-53	Miss A. Greey, J. Pinkham
1932-33	Miss M. Cook, G.S.H. Cook	1953-54	Mrs. B. Westcott, B. Westcott
1933-34	Mrs. C.A. Boone, S.F. Gundy	1954-55	Mrs. B. Westcott, B. Westcott
1934-35	Miss G. Dack, C.O. Wood	1955-56	Mrs. B. Westcott, H.E. Porter
1935-36	Miss K.E. Palm, G.G. Crean	1956-57	Mrs. B. Westcott, H.E. Porter
1936-37	Mrs. E.M. Morris, G.S.H. Cook	1957-58	Miss M. Rechnitzer, J. Pinkham
1937-38	Mrs. E.F. Coke, J.G. Crean	1958-59	Mrs. B. Westcott, J. Pequegnat
1938-39	Mrs. B.B. Geale, B.B. Geale	1959-60	Mrs. R.W. Nicholls, B. Westcott
1939-40	Mrs. E.F. Coke, J.G. Crean	1960-61	Mrs. A.G. Richmond, J. Pinkham
1940-41	Miss G. Dack, T.H. Smith	1961-62	Mrs. A.G. Richmond, J. Pinkham
1941-42	No Contest	1962-63	Miss K. Rechnitzer, J. Pinkham
1942-43	No Contest	1963-64	Miss K. Rechnitzer, J. Pinkham
1943-44	No Contest	1964-65	Miss K. Rechnitzer, J. Pinkham
1944-45	No Contest	1965-66	Miss K. Rechnitzer, J. Pinkham
1945-46	Mrs. B.B. Geale, B.B. Geale	1966-67	Mrs. H. Salmond, H.E. Porter

Year	Winners	Year	Winners
1967-68	Miss K. Rechnitzer, J.A. Pequegnat	1983-84	Susan Wansbrough & Chris Wansbrough
1968-69	Mrs. A.G. Richmond, J. Pinkham	1984-85	Susan Crossley & Chris Wansbrough
1969-70	Mrs. A.G. Richmond, J. Pinkham	1985-86	Jane Wansbrough & Chris Wansbrough
1970-71	Mrs. A.G. Richmond, J. Pinkham	1986-87	Lisa Korthals & Chris Barnard
1971-72	Mrs. A.G. Richmond, J. Pinkham	1987-88	Ann McPherson & Brodie Townley
1972-73	Miss J. Ritch, G. Mills	1988-89	Ann McPherson & Bev Westcott
1973-74	Mrs. A.G. Richmond, J. Pinkham	1989-90	Sue Sisam & Bruce Taylor
1974-75	Mrs. A.G. Richmond, J. Pinkham	1990-91	Ruth Wansbrough & Reed Ballon
1975-76	Pam Davidson & Bud Porter	1991-92	Sue Sisam & Bruce Taylor
1976-77	Ann Richmond & John Pinkham	1992-93	Sue Crossley & John Kitchen
1977-78	Ann Richmond & John Pinkham	1993-94	Sue Crossley & John Kitchen
1978-79	Susan Wansbrough & Geoff Mills	1994-95	Sue Sisam & Bruce Taylor
1979-80	Susan Wansbrough & Geoff Mills	1995-96	Sue Sisam & Bruce Taylor
1980-81	Susan Wansbrough & Geoff Mills	1996-97	Sue Sisam & Bruce Taylor
1981-82	Susan Wansbrough & Geoff Mills	1997-98	Sue Howe & Geoff Mills
1982-83	Susan Wansbrough & Chris Wansbrough	1998-99	Edith Chow & Dennis Lam

Squash

Ladies A Singles

Elizabeth Parker & Mary Taylor Trophy Presented in 1958

Year	Winner	Year	Winner
1958	Mrs. J.M. Taylor	1978-79	Susan McElhinney
1959	Mrs. J.M. Taylor	1979-80	Susan McElhinney
1960	No Contest	1980-81	Daphne Rabnett
1961	No Contest	1981-82	Pam Davidson
1962	No Contest	1982-83	Susan Behan
1963	Mrs. W. E. Parker	1983-84	Susan Behan
1964	Mrs. W. E. Parker	1984-85	Ann Thompson
1965	Mrs. W. D. Heintzman	1985-86	No Contest
1966	Mrs. W. D. Heintzman	1986-87	Susan Behan
1967	Miss W. Welch	1987-88	Pam Jarvis
1968	Miss J. Traviss	1988-89	Susan Behan
1969	Mrs. K. White	1989-90	Susan Behan
1970	Miss N. Henderson	1990-91	Susan Behan
1971	Miss N. Henderson	1991-92	Susan Behan
1972	Miss N. Henderson	1992-93	Susan Behan
1973	Miss N. Henderson	1994-95	Susan Behan
1974	Miss S. McElhinney	1995-96	Susan Behan
1975-76	Susan McElhinney	1996-97	Susan Behan
1975	Miss S. McElhinney	1997-98	Susan Behan
1976-77	Susan McElhinney	1997-98	Susan Behan
1977-78	Susan McElhinney	1998-99	Susan Behan

Squash
Ladies A Doubles

Year	Winners	Year	Winners
1984-85	Susan Behan & Moira McElhinney	1992-93	Nancy Esson & Megan Hill
1985-86	Susan Behan & Moira Goodman	1993-94	Sue Behan & Wendy Jarvis
1986-87	Brenda Harrison & Wendy Jarvis	1994-95	No contest
1987-88	Brenda Harrison & Wendy Jarvis	1995-96	No contest
1988-89	Nancy Esson & Megan Hill	1996-97	No contest
1989-90	Susan Behan & Cathy Fauquier	1997-98	No contest
1990-91	Susan Behan & Gayle Woods	1998-99	No contest
1991-92	No contest		

Squash: Softball
Men's A Singles
William R. Parker Trophy Presented in 1976

Year	Winner	Year	Winner
1976	Victor Harding	1988	Victor Harding
1977	Bill Hatch Jr.	1989	Victor Harding
1978	Victor Harding	1990	Rod Behan
1979	Bryce Hunter	1991	Victor Harding
1980	Victor Harding	1992	Victor Harding
1981	Victor Harding	1993	Hugh Baker
1982	Bryce Hunter	1994	Victor Harding
1983	Victor Harding	1995	Victor Harding
1984	Victor Harding	1996	Michael Berry
1985	Victor Harding	1997	Ian Toth
1986	Victor Harding	1998	Bruce Taylor
1987	Victor Harding	1999	Victor Harding

Squash: Hardball

Men's A Singles 70+

Mr. and Mrs. John Lash Trophy Presented in 1925

Year	Winner	Year	Winner
1925	J. C. Hope	1946	H. V. Peterson
1926	C. T. Clark	1947	J. K. McCausland
1927	W. S. Greening	1948	J. K. McCausland
1928	C. T. Clark	1949	E. Howard
1929	A. G. Poupore	1950	M. G. Jones
1930	G. B. Beatty	1951	E. Howard
1931	G. B. Beatty	1952	E. Howard
1932	J. K. McCausland	1953	E. Howard
1933	J. K. McCausland	1954	J. W. Minton
1934	C. C. Radcliffe	1955	W. Hatch
1935	J. K. McCausland	1956	E. Howard
1936	J. K. McCausland	1957	E. Howard
1937	C. C. Radcliffe	1958	E. Howard
1938	J. K. McCausland	1959	E. Howard
1939	J. K. McCausland	1960	E. Howard
1940	C. C. Radcliffe	1961	E. Howard
1941	J. K. McCausland	1962	E. Howard
1942	No Contest	1963	E. Howard
1943	No Contest	1964	J. E. Foy
1944	No Contest	1965	E. Howard
1945	No Contest	1966	D. E. Bassett

Appendix — Our Best Shots

Year	Winner	Year	Winner
1967	J. F. Bassett	1982-83	Peter Hetherington
1968	J. F. Bassett	1983-84	Bob Smart
1969	J. F. Bassett	1984-85	Victor Harding
1970	R. T. Corcoran	1985-86	Victor Harding
1971	J. E. Foy	1986-87	Victor Harding
1972	R. T. Corcoran	1987-88	Victor Harding
1973	R. T. Corcoran	1988-89	Victor Harding
1974	V. Harding	1989-90	Victor Harding
1975-76	V. Harding	1990-91	Victor Harding
1975	V. Harding	1991-92	Hugh Baker
1976-77	V. Harding	1992-93	Victor Harding
1977-78	Bill Hatch Jr.	1993-94	David Stevenson
1978-79	Victor Harding	1994-95	David Stevenson
1979-80	Victor Harding	1995-96	No Contest
1980-81	Victor Harding	1996-97	Event Retired
1981-82	Bryce Hunter		

Squash
Men's Vet A Singles 70+
D. R. Musgrave Trophy Presented in 1973

Year	Winner	Year	Winner
1963	J. W. Minton	1979-80	No Contest
1964	J. W. Minton	1980-81	No Contest
1965	W. M. Hatch, Sr.	1981-82	No Contest
1966	W. M. Hatch, Sr.	1982-83	John Pinkham
1967	W. M. Hatch, Sr.	1983-84	Mike Whelpton
1968	W. M. Hatch, Sr.	1984-85	Bill Bowen
1969	D. B. Gossage	1985-86	Mike Whelpton
1970	A. C. Wells	1986-87	Michael Gardiner
1970-71	Tony Wells	1987-88	Michael Gardiner
1971-72	John Foy	1988-89	Mike Whelpton
1972-73	Peter Stewart	1989-90	Michael Gardiner
1973-74	John Foy	1990-91	Michael Gardiner
1974-75	John Foy	1991-92	Michael Gardiner
1975-76	John Foy	1992-93	Michael Gardiner
1976-77	No Contest	1993-94	Michael Gardiner
1977-78	No Contest	1994-95	Michael Gardiner
1978-79	No Contest		

Squash
Men's Vet A Singles Softball
Philip J. Hanley Trophy Presented in 1963

Year	Winner	Year	Winner
1963	J. W. Minton	1981-82	Terry Corcoran
1964	J. W. Minton	1982-83	Terry Corcoran
1965	Wm. Hatch Sr.	1983-84	Michael Whelpton
1966	Wm. Hatch Sr.	1984-85	Terry Corcoran
1967	Wm. Hatch Sr.	1985-86	Terry Corcoran
1968	Wm. Hatch Sr.	1986-87	Michael Gardiner
1969	D. B. Gossage	1987-88	Bryce Hunter
1970	A. C. Wells	1988-89	Michael Gardiner
1971	A. C. Wells	1989-90	John Boynton
1972	J. E. Foy	1990-91	John Boynton
1973	P. M. Steewart	1991-92	Michael Gardiner
1974	J. E. Foy	1992-93	Michael Gardiner
1975	J. E. Foy	1993-94	Michael Gardiner
1976	J. E. Foy	1994-95	Michael Gardiner
1976-77	Terry Corcoran	1995-96	Peter Hatcher
1977-78	Terry Corcoran	1996-97	Peter Hatcher
1978-79	Terry Corcoran	1997-98	No Contest
1979-80	Terry Corcoran	1998-99	No Contest
1980-81	Terry Corcoran		

Squash

Men's A Doubles

J.K. McCausland Trophy

Year	Winner(s)	Year	Winner(s)
1963	H. John C. Ireton, D. Leggat	1981-82	Peter Hatcher & Peter Hetherington
1964	J. E. Foy, P. M. Stewart	1982-83	Bryce Hunter & Steve McIntyre
1965	J. E. Foy, P. M. Stewart	1983-84	John Boynton & Mark Pigott
1966	J. E. Foy, P. M. Stewart	1984-85	Bryce Hunter & Steve McIntyre
1967	D. Leggat, E. W. Whelpton	1985-86	Bryce Hunter & Steve McIntyre
1968	J. E. Foy, P. M. Stewart	1986-87	Stu Boynton & Victor Harding
1969	J. E. Foy, P. M. Stewart	1987-88	Stu Boynton & Victor Harding
1970	J. E. Foy, P. M. Stewart	1988-89	Stu Boynton & Victor Harding
1971	J. E. Foy, P. M. Stewart	1989-90	John Boynton & Peter Hetherington
1972	J. E. Foy, P. M. Stewart	1990-91	Hugh Baker & Victor Harding
1973	A. Massey, P. Seagram	1991-92	Hugh Baker & Victor Harding
1974	D. Leggat, T. McCarthy	1992-93	John Boynton & John Greenwood
1975	V. Harding, L. McCarthy	1993-94	Hugh Baker & Victor Harding
1975-76	Victor Harding & Leighton McCarthy	1994-95	John Boynton & John Greenwood
1976-77	Terry Corcoran & Bryce Hunter	1995-96	Hugh Baker & Victor Harding
1977-78	Don Leggatt & Tom McCarthy	1996-97	Hugh Baker & Victor Harding
1978-79	Bryce Hunter & Steve McIntyre	1997-98	Reed Ballon & David Stevenson
1979-80	Bryce Hunter & Steve McIntyre	1998-99	Reed Ballon & David Stevenson
1980-81	Bryce Hunter & Steve McIntyre		

Squash
Men's Veteran Doubles
Christie T. Clarke Trophy Presented in 1957

Year	Winner(s)	Year	Winner(s)
1957	T. D. Boynton & D. B. Hamilton	1978-79	John Foy & Richard Seagram
1958	T. D. Boynton & D. B. Hamilton	1979-80	John Blaikie & Bill Parker Jr.
1959	T. D. Boynton & D. B. Hamilton	1980-81	Tom Dancy & Don Leggat
1960	T. D. Boynton & D. B. Hamilton	1981-82	John Foy & Richard Seagram
1961	T. D. Boynton & D. B. Hamilton	1982-83	Terry Corcoran & Peter Hatcher
1962	T. D. Boynton & D. B. Hamilton	1983-84	Terry Corcoran & Peter Hatcher
1963	T.D. Boynton & D. B. Hamilton	1984-85	Richard Seagram & Mike Whelpton
1964	T.D. Boynton & D. B. Hamilton	1985-86	Terry Corcoran & Bryce Hunter
1965	T.D. Boynton & D. B. Hamilton	1986-87	Terry Corcoran & Bryce Hunter
1966	R. D. Jennings & D. S. Mills	1987-88	Terry Corcoran & Bryce Hunter
1967	R. D. Jennings & D. S. Mills	1988-89	Richard Seagram & Mike Whelpton
1968	E. W. Whelpton & M. G. Jones	1989-90	John Boynton & Mark Pigott
1969	J. W. Minton & L.J.H. Gunn	1990-91	No contest
1970	W. M. Hatch Sr.& J. W. Minton	1991-92	John Boynton & Mark Pigott
1971	E. W. Whelpton & W. D. Whitaker	1992-93	John Boynton & Mark Pigott
1972	J. E. Foy & P. M. Stewart	1993-94	Peter Hatcher & Bryce Hunter
1973	T. Dancy & D. Leggat	1994-95	Peter Hatcher & Bryce Hunter
1974	J. E. Foy & P. M. Stewart	1995-96	Peter Hatcher & Bryce Hunter
1975	J. E. Foy & P. M. Stewart	1996-97	Jeff Osborne & John Wright
1975-76	John Foy & Peter Stewart	1997-98	Peter Hatcher & Bryce Hunter
1976-77	Terry Corcoran & Tom Dancy	1998-99	Greg Young & Geoff Osborne
1977-78	John Foy & Richard Seagram		

Squash
Men's Senior Doubles
H. V. Petersen Trophy Presented in 1965

Year	Winner(s)	Year	Winner(s)
1965	C. M. Burgess & M. O'Grady	1982-83	Bud Cooper & Tony Wells
1966	G.N. Fisher & P. Henderson	1983-84	Murray Sullivan & Noel Wittick
1967	J. C. Stewart & P. K. Hanley	1984-85	Tom Dancy & Don Leggat
1968	M. O'Grady & C. M. Burgess	1985-86	Tom Dancy & Don Leggat
1969	J. S. Boynton & W. M. Hatch Jr.	1986-87	Terry Corcoran & Tony Wells
1970	D. G. Bassett & K. Langmuir	1987-88	Robin Logie & Richard Seagram
1971	P. R. Griffin & R.C. W. Logie	1988-89	Robin Logie & Richard Seagram
1972	D. G. Bassett & K. M. Langmuir	1989-90	Robin Logie & Richard Seagram
1973	A. Bolte & J. Jennings	1990-91	Peter Berry & Tom Dancy
1974	D. G. Bassett & K. Langmuir	1991-92	Robin Logie & Richard Seagram
1975	J. Deeks & G. Young	1992-93	Robin Logie & Richard Seagram
1975-76	Peter Berry & Peter Griffin	1993-94	No contest
1976-77	Peter Berry & Peter Griffin	1994-95	Norm Seagram & Mike Whelpton
1977-78	Peter Berry & Peter Griffin	1995-96	Howie Rober & Robin Logie
1978-79	Bud Cooper & Tony Wells	1996-97	Robin Logie & Howie Rober
1979-80	Bud Cooper & Tony Wells	1997-98	Robin Logie & Howie Rober
1980-81	Bud Cooper & Tony Wells	1998-99	Robin Logie & Howie Rober
1981-82	Bob Bertram & Aug Bolte		

Squash
Men's Master Doubles
August A. Bolte Trophy Presented in 1994

Year	Winner(s)	Year	Winner(s)
1988-89	Aug Bolte & Murray Sullivan	1994-95	Robin Logie & Howie Rober
1989-90	Peter Berry & Tom Dancy	1995-96	No contest
1990-91	No contest	1996-97	Howie Rober & Robin Logie
1991-92	Don Leggat & Noel Wittick	1997-98	Norm Seagram & Richard Seagram
1992-93	Don Leggat & Noel Wittick	1998-99	Robin Logie & Howie Rober
1993-94	Robin Logie & Jack Mollenhauer		

Squash
Mixed A Doubles

Year	Winner(s)	Year	Winner(s)
1986-87	Sue Behan & Rod Behan	1993-94	Gayle Woods & Victor Harding
1987-88	Nancy Esson & Victor Harding	1994-95	Gayle Woods & Victor Harding
1988-89	Wendy Jarvis & David Jarvis	1995-96	Gayle Woods & Victor Harding
1989-90	Pam Davidson & John Boynton	1996-97	Gayle Woods & Victor Harding
1990-91	Gayle Woods & Victor Harding	1997-98	Gayle Woods & Victor Harding
1991-92	No contest	1998-99	Gayle Woods & Victor Harding
1992-93	Gayle Woods & Victor Harding		

Tennis
Ladies A Singles
Mildred C. Brock Trophy

Year	Winner(s)	Year	Winner(s)
1938	Miss M. Waldie	1959	Mrs. F. D. Lace
1939	Miss M. Withers	1960	Mrs. F. D. Lace
1940	Miss P. Macabe	1961	Miss. B. Nunns
1941	Miss P. Macabe	1962	Miss. B. Nunns
1942	No Contest	1963	Miss. B. Nunns
1943	No Contest	1964	Miss J. Traviss
1944	No Contest	1965	Miss B. Nunns
1945	No Contest	1966	Miss B. Nunns
1946	Miss M. Withers	1967	Mrs. W. D. Heintzman
1947	Mrs. G. Nunns	1968	Mrs. W. D. Heintzman
1948	Mrs. K. Salmond	1969	Mrs. W. D. Heintzman
1949	Mrs. K . Salmond	1970	Miss J. Traviss
1950	Mrs. K . Salmond	1971	Miss J. Traviss
1951	Mrs. F. D. Lace	1972	Mrs. W. D. Heintzman
1952	Miss D. Proctor	1973	Miss S. Wansbrough
1953	Miss M. Nunns	1974	Pam O'Rorke
1954	Miss M. Nunns	1975	Barbara Heintzman
1955	Miss M. Nunns	1976	Barbara Heintzman
1956	Miss M. Nunns	1977	Nancy Doherty
1957	Mrs. F. D. Lace	1978	Nancy Doherty
1958	Miss B. Nunns	1979	Brenda Davidson

Year	Winner	Year	Winner
1980	Nancy Doherty	1990	Jane Philp
1981	Nancy Doherty	1991	Cynthia Mitchell
1982	Penny McLeod	1992	Cynthia Mitchell
1983	Penny McLeod	1993	Jane Philp
1984	Penny McLeod	1994	Jane Philp
1985	Penny McLeod	1995	Cynthia Mitchell
1986	Penny McLeod	1996	Cynthia Mitchell
1987	Penny McLeod	1997	Laura Jewett
1988	Jane Philp	1998	Laura Jewett
1989	Jane Philp	1999	Laura Jewett

Tennis
Ladies A Doubles
Mrs. H. Plaxton Trophy Presented in 1949

Year	Winner(s)	Year	Winner(s)
1938	Mrs. E. F. Coke, Mrs. F. Risdon	1959	Mrs. G. Nunns, Miss R. Nunns
1939	Miss M. Brock, Mrs E. F. Coke	1960	Mrs. G. Nunns, Mrs. H. Salmond
1940	Mrs. E. F. Coke, Miss M. Brock	1961	Miss B. Nunns, Miss R. Nunns
1941	Miss M. Brock, Mrs E. F. Coke	1962	Miss B. Nunns, Miss R. Nunns
1942	No Contest	1963	Mrs. F. H. Fisher & Mrs. H. Salmond
1943	No Contest	1964	Mrs. F. H. Fisher & Mrs. H. Salmond
1944	No Contest	1965	Mrs. F. H. Fisher & Mrs. H. Salmond
1945	No Contest	1966	Mrs. C. D. Suydam & Miss J. Traviss
1946	Miss. M. Withers, Mrs J. R. Frith	1967	Mrs. J. R. Evans & Mrs. J. F. Howard
1947	Mrs. F. D. Lace, Mrs. G. Nunns	1968	Mrs. H. Salmond & Mrs. R. Fisher
1948	Mrs. J. K. McCausland, Mrs. K. Salmond	1969	Mrs. J. R. Evans & Mrs J. F. Howard
1949	Mrs. F. D. Lace, Mrs. G. Nunns	1970	Mrs. H. Salmond & Mrs. R. Fisher
1950	Mrs. G. Nunns, Mrs. K Salmond	1971	Mrs. H. Salmond & Mrs. R. Fisher
1951	Mrs. K. Salmond, Mrs. G. Nunns	1972	Mrs. H. Salmond & Mrs. R. Fisher
1952	Mrs. H. Macdonnell, Mrs. K. Salmond	1973	Mrs. H. Salmond & Mrs. R. Fisher
1953	Mrs. G. Nunns, Miss M. Nunns	1974	Mrs. K. Grant & Mrs. P. Northey
1954	Mrs. G. Nunns, Miss M. Nunns	1975	Ruby Fisher & Hope Salmond
1955	Mrs. G. Nunns, Miss M. Nunns	1976	Barbara Heintzman & Bea Nunns
1956	Mrs. G. Nunns, Miss M. Nunns	1977	Ruby Fisher & Hope Salmond
1957	Mrs. G. Nunns, Miss M. Nunns	1978	Nancy Doherty & Ruth Grant
1958	Mrs. R. Macdonnell, Mrs. H. Salmond	1979	Nancy Doherty & Ruth Grant

Year	Winners	Year	Winners
1980	Anne Nichols & Pam O'Rorke	1992	Nancy Doherty & Ruth Grant
1981	Nancy Doherty & Ruth Grant	1992	Nancy Doherty & Ruth Grant
1984	Nancy Doherty & Ruth Grant	1993	Nancy Doherty & Ruth Grant
1985	Nancy Doherty & Ruth Grant	1993	Sue Crossley & Jane Philp
1986	Nancy Doherty & Ruth Grant	1994	Abigail Abouchar & Nancy Doherty
1987	Nancy Doherty & Ruth Grant	1995	Anne Churchill-Smith & Cathy Wright
1988	Nancy Doherty & Ruth Grant	1996	AnneChurchill-Smith & Cathy Wright
1989	No Contest	1997	Anne Churchill-Smith & Cathy Wright
1990	Nancy Doherty & Ruth Grant	1998	Laura Jewett & Abigail Abouchar
1991	Nancy Doherty & Ruth Grant	1999	Laura Jewett & Abigail Abouchar

Margot Northey, Mary Gordon, Ruby Fisher, Hope Salmond — tennis.

Tennis
Ladies Senior Doubles

Year	Winner(s)	Year	Winner(s)
1982	Ruby Fisher & Hope Salmond	1991	No Contest
1983	Barbara Langfeldt & Jane Mustard	1992	Annabelle Heintzman & Anne McLeod
1984	Marg Knutson & Hope Salmond	1993	Pat Davidson & Sarah Lafleur
1985	Marg Knutson & Hope Salmond	1994	Annabelle Heintzman & Anne McLeod
1986	Marg Knutson & Hope Salmond	1995	Kathy Crossgrove & Judy Meredith
1987	Marg Knutson & Hope Salmond	1996	Honor Shepley & Marnie Wigle
1988	Barbara Langfeldt & Jane Mustard	1997	Di Tweedy & Pat Davidson
1989	No Contest	1998	Honor Shepley & Marnie Wigle
1990	Barbara Langfeldt & Jane Mustard	1999	Honor Shepley & Marnie Wigle

Tennis

Men's A Singles

Henry Hewetson Trophy Presented in 1949

Year	Winner	Year	Winner
1939	F. W. Torrance	1960	J. Bassett Jr.
1940	Dr. A. W. Ham	1961	P. M. Stewart
1941	B. Harris	1962	M. Gibson
1942	W. T. Pinkerton	1963	M. Gibson
1943	No Contest	1964	J. F. Bassett
1944	No Contest	1965	J. Foy
1945	No Contest	1966	D. E. Bassett
1946	No Contest	1967	P. Barnard
1947	D. Dyment	1968	P. Barnard
1948	J. W. Minton	1969	H. E. Fauquier
1949	R. D. Murray	1970	H. E. Fauquier
1950	M. G. Jones	1971	H. E. Fauquier
1951	C. Clark Hopper	1972	H. E. Fauquier
1952	C. C.ark Hopper	1973	H. E. Fauquier
1953	J. W. Minton	1974	Peter Barnard
1954	G. Nunns	1975	Tom McCarthy
1955	P. Stewart	1976	Harry Fauquier
1956	P. Stewart	1977	Peter Barnard
1957	J. Bassett 3rd	1978	Peter Barnard
1958	M. G. Jones	1979	Peter Barnard
1959	P. Stewart	1980	Peter Hatcher

Appendix — Our Best Shots

Year	Winner	Year	Winner
1981	Greg Halder	1991	Stephen Hunter
1982	Greg Halder	1992	Richard Thompsom
1983	Harry Fauquier	1993	Stephen Hunter
1984	Peter Hatcher	1994	Stephen Hunter
1985	Peter Hatcher	1995	Stephen Hunter
1986	Peter Hatcher	1996	Stephen Hunter
1987	Bob Bedard	1997	Stephen Hunter
1988	Stephen Hunter	1998	Stephen Hunter
1989	No Contest	1999	Tim Griffin
1990	Peter Hatcher		

Peter Barnard, Dave McPherson, Stephen Hunter — tennis.

Tennis
Men's Senior A Singles
H. V. Petersen Trophy Presented in 1967

Year	Winner	Year	Winner
1967	W. E. Halder	1984	Robin Logie
1968	W. E. Halder	1985	Robin Logie
1969	W. E. Halder	1986	Robin Logie
1970	W. E. Halder	1987	Bob Armstrong
1971	W. E. Halder	1988	Robin Logie
1972	W. E. Halder	1989	No Contest
1973	Peter Griffin	1990	Robin Logie
1974	Murray Young	1991	Robin Logie
1975	Peter Griffin	1992	Robin Logie
1976	Peter Griffin	1993	Terry Whelpton
1977	John Foy	1994	Terry Whelpton
1978	Robin Logie	1995	Terrry Whelpton
1979	Robin Logie	1996	Robin Logie
1980	Robin Logie	1997	Tim Griffin
1981	Robin Logie	1998	Robin Logie
1982	Robin Logie	1999	Tim Griffin
1983	Robin Logie		

Tennis
Men's Master Singles

Year	Winner	Year	Winner
1991	Tony Wells	1996	Robin Logie
1992	Tony Wells	1997	Robin Logie
1993	Robin Logie	1998	Robin Logie
1994	Robin Logie	1999	Robin Logie
1995	Robin Logie		

Robin Logie, Chris Wansbrough, Peter Gordon, Pat Northey — tennis.

Tennis
Men's A Doubles
John S. Proctor Trophy

Year	Winner	Year	Winner
1938	A. W. Baille & Dr. A. W. Ham	1959	J. Bassett Sr. & P. Stewart
1939	B. Harrison & D. K. Hanley	1960	J. W. H. Bassett P. M. Stewart
1940	B. Harrison & D. K. Hanley	1961	J. Foy & M. Jones
1941	H. H. Hewetson & J. K. McCausland	1962	M. Gibson & J. P. Northey
1942	No contest	1963	J. P. Northey & P. M. Stewart
1943	No contest	1964	P. B. Barnard & D. G. Brock
1944	No contest	1965	R. C. Logie & J. P. Northey
1945	No contest	1966	J. W. H. Bassett & J. F. Bassett
1946	J. K. McCausland & H. H. Hewetson	1967	P. Barnard & D. G. Brock
1947	A. Y. Eaton & D. B. Hamilton	1968	J. F. Bassett & P. Barnard
1948	C. Hopper & M. Jones	1969	J. F. Bassett & P. Barnard
1949	C. Hopper & M. Jones	1970	Harry Fauquier & Tom McCarthy
1950	C. Hopper & M. Jones	1971	Harry Fauquier & Tom McCarthy
1951	C. Hopper & M. Jones	1972	Harry Fauquier & Tom McCarthy
1952	C. Hop per & M. Jones	1973	Harry Fauquier & Tom McCarthy
1953	C. Hopper & M. Jones	1974	Harry Fauquier & Tom McCarthy
1954	C. Hopper & M. Jones	1975	Harry Fauquier & Tom McCarthy
1955	J. Bassett Sr. & P. Stewart	1976	Peter Barnard & Peter Hatcher
1956	J. Foy & W. Halder	1977	Peter Barnard & Peter Hatcher
1957	J. Bassett Sr. & P. Stewart	1978	Harry Fauquier & Tom McCarthy
1958	J. Bassett Sr. & P. Stewart	1979	Harry Fauquier & Tom McCarthy

Year	Winners	Year	Winners
1980	Peter Barnard & Peter Hatcher	1990	Peter Barnard & Stephen Hunter
1981	Peter Barnard & Peter Hatcher	1991	Peter Barnard & Stephen Hunter
1982	Greg Halder & Wally Halder	1992	Stephen Hunter & Sandy Logie
1983	Peter Barnard & Peter Hatcher	1993	Stephen Hunter & Sandy Logie
1984	Peter Barnard & Peter Hatcher	1994	Stephen Hunter & Sandy Logie
1985	Robin Logie & Sandy Logie	1995	Stephen Hunter & Sandy Logie
1986	Roger Rowan & Richard Woods	1996	Martin Walker & Peter Hatcher
1987	Peter Hatcher & Martin Walker	1997	Robin Logie & Will Drope
1988	Roger Rowan & Richard Woods	1998	Stephen Hunter & Sandy Logie
1989	No Contest	1999	Tim Griffin & Adrian Griffin

Tennis

Men's Senior A Doubles

Murray Garden Trophy Presented in 1966

Year	Winner(s)	Year	Winner(s)
1964	J. W. H. Bassett & R. H. Winters	1982	Robin Logie & Richard Seagram
1965	J. W. H. Bassett & R. H. Winters	1983	Robin Logie & Richard Seagram
1966	F. B. Harrison & W. H. Reid	1984	Chuck Baird & Frank Dimock
1967	W. E. Halder & M. G. Jones	1985	Chuck Baird & Frank Dimock
1968	W. E. Halder & M. G. Jones	1986	Robin Logie & Richard Seagram
1969	F. M. Young & P. Griffin	1987	Pat Northey & Martin Walker
1970	F. M. Young & P. Griffin	1988	Robin Logie & Richard Seagram
1971	F. M. Young & P. Griffin	1989	No Contest
1972	W. E. Halder & F. M. Young	1990	Robin Logie & Richard Seagram
1973	W. E. Halder & F. M. Young	1991	Robin Logie & Richard Seagram
1974	W. E. Halder & F. M. Young	1992	Robin Logie & Richard Seagram
1975	Jim Barclay & Murray Young	1993	Martin Walker & Terry Whelpton
1976	Bruce Harrison & Roy Mansell	1994	Mike Innes & Jack Way
1977	Peter Griffin & Murray Young	1995	Mike Innes & Jack Way
1978	Peter Griffin & Robin Logie	1996	Martin Walker & Pat Northey
1979	John Foy & Peter Stewart	1997	Peter Barnard & Chris Wansbrough
1980	Norman Atkins & Pat Northey	1998	Peter Barnard & Chris Wansbrough
1981	Peter Griffin & Robin Logie	1999	Paul Emond & Terry Whelpton

Tennis
Men's Master Doubles
Wally Halder Trophy Presented in 1994

Year	Winner(s)	Year	Winner(s)
1981	Bruce Harrison & Roy Mansell	1991	Terry Wardrop & Tony Wells
1982	Peter Griffin & Murray Young	1992	Terry Wardrop & Tony Wells
1983	Peter Griffin & Murray Young	1993	Robin Logie & Chris Wansbrough
1984	Charles Baird & Frank Dimock	1994	Robin Logie & Chris Wansbrough
1985	Charles Baird & Frank Dimock	1995	Robin Logie & Chris Wansbrough
1986	Frank Dimock & Gord Farquharson	1996	Peter Gordon & Pat Northey
1987	Frank Dimock & Gord Farquharson	1997	Robin Logie & Chris Wansbrough
1988	Frank Dimock & Gord Farquharson	1998	Robin Logie & Chris Wansbrough
1989	No Contest	1999	Robin Logie & Chris Wansbrough
1990	Terry Wardrop & Tony Wells		

Tennis
Men's Over 70 Doubles
The Harrison Trophy Presented in 1988

Year	Winner(s)	Year	Winner(s)
1988	Bruce Harrison & Roy Mansell	1994	Meredith Fleming & Joe Nixon
1989	No Contest	1995	R.D. Grant & Murray Young
1990	Bruce Harrison & Roy Mansell	1996	Ed Ballon & Blair Fergusson
1991	Wally Halder & Murray Young	1997	Ed Ballon & Blair Fergusson
1992	Wally Halder & Murray Young	1998	Bob Langmuir & Murray Young
1993	Wally Halder & Murray Young	1999	Bob Langmuir & Murray Young

Tennis
Men's Over 80 Doubles
Elliott Dalton Trophy Presented in 1994

Year	Winner(s)	Year	Winner(s)
1994	W.D. Sanderson & George Heintzman	1998	R.D. Grant & St.Clair Balfour
1996	Ramsey Fraser & A.G.S. Griffin	1999	R.D. Grant & W.D. Sanderson
1997	Ramsey Fraser & A.G.S. Griffin		

W.D. Sanderson, George Heintzman with the Over 80 tennis trophy, presented by Marie Dalton in memory of her husband.

Tennis
Mixed A Doubles
G. T. Peppal Trophy

Year	Winner(s)	Year	Winner(s)
1938	Mrs. E. F. Coke, Dr. A. W. Ham	1959	Miss Margot Nunns, P. Stewart
1939	Miss M. Brock, F. W. Torrance	1960	Miss R. Nunns, J. Foy
1940	Mrs. E. F. Coke, G. G. Rolph	1961	Miss R. Nunns, J. Foy
1941	Miss P. McCabe, J. K. McCausland	1962	Miss R. Nunns, J. Foy
1942	No contest	1963	Miss B. Nunns & D. G. Brock
1943	No contest	1964	Miss B. Nunns & P. Northey
1944	No contest	1965	Miss J. Traviss & D. E. Bassett
1945	No contest	1966	Mrs. R. Grant & J. E. Foy
1946	Miss C. Kilgour, K. Dyment	1967	Miss J. Traviss & P. M. Stewart
1947	Miss M. Brock, F. W. Torrance	1968	Mrs. R. Fisher & P. M. Stewart
1948	Mrs. G. Nunns, A. Y. Eaton	1969	Mrs. R. Fisher & P. M. Stewart
1949	Mrs. K. Salmond, H. V. Petersen	1970	Mrs. R. Fisher & P. M. Stewart
1950	Mrs. K. Salmond, H. V. Petersen	1971	Miss J. Traviss & T. McCarthy
1951	Mrs. K Salmond, F. W. Torrance	1972	Mrs. R. Fisher & P. M. Stewart
1952	Mrs. G. Nunns, M. G. Jones	1973	Mrs. R. Fisher & P. M. Stewart
1953	Mrs. K. Salmond, C. Hopper	1974	Mrs. R. Fisher & P. M. Stewart
1954	Mrs. G. Nunns, M. G. Jones	1975	Mrs. R. Fisher & P. M. Stewart
1955	Miss M. Nunns, P. Stewart	1976	No contest
1956	Miss M. Nunns, P. Stewart	1977	No contest
1957	Miss Margot Nunns, P. Stewart	1978	No contest
1958	Miss R. Nunns, J. Foy	1979	No contest

Year	Winners	Year	Winners
1980	No contest	1990	Jane Philp & Chris Wansbrough
1981	No contest	1991	Cynthia Mitchell & Hugh Baker
1982	No contest	1992	Cynthia Mitchell & Hugh Baker
1983	No contest	1993	Cynthia Mitchell & Hugh Baker
1984	No contest	1994	Cynthia Mitchell & Hugh Baker
1985	Penny McLeod & Richard Woods	1995	Cynthia Mitchell & Hugh Baker
1986	Penny McLeod & Richard Woods	1996	Jane Philp & Chris Wansbrough
1987	Penny McLeod & Richard Woods	1997	Laura Jewett & Sandy Logie
1988	Jane Philp & Chris Wansbrough	1998	Laura Jewett & Sandy Logie
1989	No contest	1999	Laura Jewett & Sandy Logie

Future champs.

Platform Tennis
Ladies A Doubles

Year	Winners	Year	Winners
1975-76	Mary Gordon & Ruth Grant	1987-88	Nancy Doherty & Pam O'Rorke
1976-77	Pat Prendergast & Jane Prendergast	1988-89	Nancy Doherty & Pam O'Rorke
1977-78	Mary Gordon & Margot Northey	1989-90	Nancy Doherty & Pam O'Rorke
1978-79	Nancy Doherty & Ann Richmond	1990-91	Anne Nichols & Sheri Fell
1979-80	Anne Nichols & Pam O'Rorke	1991-92	Nancy Doherty & Pam O'Rorke
1980-81	Pam O'Rorke & Margot Northey	1992-93	Nancy Doherty & Pam O'Rorke
1981-82	Anne Nichols & Nancy Doherty	1993-94	Nancy Doherty & Pam O'Rorke
1982-83	Pam O'Rorke & Anne Nichols	1994-95	Nancy Doherty & Pam O'Rorke
1983-84	Pam O'Rorke & Anne Nichols	1995-96	Abigail Abouchar & Brenda Northey
1984-85	Nancy Doherty & Pam O'Rorke	1996-97	Abigail Abouchar & Brenda Northey
1985-86	Nancy Doherty & Pam O'Rorke	1997-98	Joy Waldie & Brenda Northey
1986-87	Nancy Doherty & Pam O'Rorke	1998-99	Abigail Abouchar & Brenda Northey

Abigail Abouchar, Laura Jewett, Katie Wright, Cathy Southey, Anne Churchill-Smith.

Platform Tennis
Men's A Doubles

Year	Winners	Year	Winners
1975-76	Pat Northey & Peter Gordon	1987-88	Peter Hatcher & Phil MacDonnell
1976-77	Peter Hatcher & Phil MacDonnell	1988-89	Peter Hatcher & Phil MacDonnell
1977-78	Peter Hatcher & Phil MacDonnell	1989-90	Pat Northey & Martin Walker
1978-79	Peter Hatcher & Phil MacDonnell	1990-91	Pat Northey & Martin Walker
1979-80	Peter Hatcher & Phil MacDonnell	1991-92	No Contest
1980-81	Pat Northey & Peter Hatcher	1992-93	Martin Walker & Pat Northey
1981-82	Phil Macdonnell & Peter Gordon	1993-94	Hugh Baker & Terry Whelpton
1982-83	J.B. Harrison & David Jarvis	1994-95	Peter Hatcher & Phil MacDonnell
1983-84	Peter Hatcher & Phil MacDonnell	1995-96	Martin Walker & Pat Northey
1984-85	Peter Hatcher & Phil MacDonnell	1996-97	Martin Walker & Pat Northey
1985-86	Peter Hatcher & Phil MacDonnell	1997-98	John Waldie & Bruce Taylor
1986-87	Pat Northey & Martin Walker	1998-99	John Waldie & Eric Drinkwater

Martin Walker, Pat Northey, Sandy McIntosh, Eric Drinkwater — platform tennis.

Platform Tennis

Mixed A Doubles

Year	Winners	Year	Winners
1975-76	Ruth Grant & Doug Grant	1987-88	Pam O'Rorke & Martin Walker
1976-77	Mary Gordon & Peter Gordon	1988-89	Pam O'Rorke & Martin Walker
1977-78	Mary Gordon & Peter Gordon	1989-90	Pam O'Rorke & Martin Walker
1978-79	Mary Gordon & Peter Gordon	1990-91	Pam O'Rorke & Martin Walker
1979-80	Margot Northey & Pat Northey	1991-92	Nancy Doherty & Brit Doherty
1980-81	Nancy Doherty & Brit Doherty	1992-93	Pam O'Rorke & Martin Walker
1981-82	Margot Northey & Pat Northey	1993-94	Pam O'Rorke & Martin Walker
1982-8	Ruth Grant & Doug Grant	1994-95	Pam O'Rorke & Martin Walker
1983-84	Nancy Doherty & Brit Doherty	1995-96	Brenda Northey & Bruce Taylor
1984-85	Margot Northey & Pat Northey	1996-97	Abigail Abouchar & Martin Walker
1985-86	Margot Northey & Pat Northey	1997-98	Joy Waldie & John Waldie
1986-87	Pam O'Rorke & Martin Walker	1998-99	Abigail Abouchar & Terry Whelpton

Joy Waldie, Brenda Northey, Anne Churchill-Smith, Laura Jewett — platform tennis.

Dominoes Champions

Year	Singles	Doubles	Year	Singles	Doubles
1965	J.O. Shields	J.A. Hanley / H.V. Peterson	1977	D. Redfern	J. Greey / P. Gooderham
1966	H.H. Gilbert	J.A. Hanley / H.V. Peterson	1978	D. Redfern	J. Hay / P. Eckardt
1967	S.F. Gundy	No Contest	1979	D. Redfern	D. Redfern / H.H. Gilbert
1968	J.O. Shields	No Contest			
1969	R.A MacKinnon	No Contest	1980	P.S. Gooderham	W. Morris / B.B. Westcott
1970	J.A. Hanley	S.F. Gundy / R.A. MacKinnon	1981	S.F. Gundy	R. MacKinnon / S.F. Gundy
1971	J.O. Shields	D. Redfern / H.H. Gilbert	1982	P. MacDonnell	J. Pinkham / James Barclay
1972	J.A. Hanley	D. Redfern / H.H. Gilbert	1983	H.H. Gilbert	R. Farquarson / P. MacDonnell
1973	H.H. Gilbert	J. Greey / P. Gooderham	1984	R. A. MacKinnon	D. Redfern / H.H. Gilbert
1974	H.H. Gilbert	J. Shields / E. Huycke	1985	H.H. Gilbert	C. Seagram / J. Shortley
1975	D. Redfern	S.F. Gundy / R. MacKinnon	1986	B. Weston	D. Redfern / H.H. Gilbert
1976	R. MacKinnon	W.M. Morris / B.B. Westcott			

Year	Singles	Doubles	Year	Singles	Doubles
1987	G.D. Hunter	S.F. Gundy B.B. Westcott	1994	R. Bertram	R. Seagram J. Blaikie
1988	H.H. Gilbert	J.E. Deeks P.H. Gooderham Jr	1995	B.B. Westcott	R. Seagram J. Blaikie
1989	G.D. Hunter	J.G. Greey P.H. Gooderham Jr	1996	H.H. Gilbert	R.G. Seagram J.R. Blaikie
1990	H.H. Gilbert	W.L. Heisey B. Burns	1997	P.H. Gooderham	P.H. Gooderham J.G. Greey
1991	S. Watt	C. Seagram D.C. O'Kell	1998	G.D. Deeks	R.G. Seagram J.R. Blaikie
1992	G.D. Hunter	C. Seagram D.C. O'Kell	1999	P.S. Gooderham	J.G. Greey P.S. Gooderham
1993	J. Hunter	R. Seagram J. Blaikie			

Acknowledgements

I must confess that when I received a message asking me to call David Brightling in the B&R office, my first thought was that my account was overdue. When I found out that I was being asked to sum up seventy-five years of the history of this remarkable club, I was overwhelmed by the thought of doing justice to the subject — to the feats of the many outstanding members, past and present, of the Badminton and Racquet Club of Toronto. I still am. I would like to thank the seventy-fifth anniversary committee under chairman Bill Munro, and Don Moffatt, president at the time of the anniversary, for presenting me with this challenge and giving me this honour.

And now to try to thank Heather Ballon. I had worked with Heather on *Havergal, Celebrating a Century*, the history of Havergal College, and so I knew her bright efficiency, her inventiveness, her habit of doing things now instead of tomorrow, of being a first rate detective, setting herself on the trail of a fact or a story and never letting go until she had the answer, and of persisting in any seemingly endless task. An example of this was her diligent reading of seventy-five years of board minutes, a study that resulted in a summary of the most important parts of each meeting. This was invaluable to me, if a bit mind-numbing for her. I also knew that we would have a lot of laughs, essential in a pursuit that sometimes seems daunting. All of this was confirmed again. It had been often said. "I couldn't have done it without her." Here there is no doubt about it.

I would like to thank Ernie Howard, who encouraged me in my work, beginning with the decision to take on the task, met with me several times to answer questions, or to give his opinion if asked, and was always at the other end of the phone. Ernie read a draft of the book at my request to check for errors or omissions. That draft was also read by long-time members Bev Westcott, John Foy, Annabelle Heintzman, and Barbara Proctor, (both of whom have laboured long over the club's archives), as well as Heather, and, of course, her tennis partner and "captain of the team," Eddie, who was always ready with a quip at any time of the day. Heather and Annabelle have spent many hours going through old photographs to choose those that best expressed the past and present life of the club. Another great piece of detective work was done by Maggie Corcoran, who extracted information from the club's old scrapbooks for the seventy-fifth anniversary placemats — these notices have been useful as reminders of special events. In the pro shop Eleanor O'Gorman and Paul Dunning and their staff responded readily to requests for help in compiling the lists in the appendix, of trophy winners, and champions, and answered interminable questions as well.

President Warren Moysey kindly read the draft in the midst of a busy schedule organizing work at the club, as the car barns take on a new look for the last quarter of their century. The current board became involved in decisions about publication and I thank them for their interest. I talked at length to board members Wendy Jarvis and Doug Bower and appreciated their input.

It was a pleasure to have John de Visser, an associate in several books, take photographs of the club's key rooms.

My thanks go to all those who sent in suggestions for the title. In the end we decided to stay with a simple title that tells it the way it is. And so *The B&R at 75. A History of the Badminton and Racquet Club 1924-1999* was the choice. Thanks to Mrs. Mary Richardson for this. Some of the other suggestions, however, seemed to fit certain sections and so Patty Boake, Eddie Ballon, and Ann Richmond will find their titles used. There are about eighty other people to thank, those who met with me and my tape recorder for lively interviews. What I heard more often than not was "I know a good story, but of course you couldn't print it." And they were right. Some were certainly unprintable. But from these chats the life of the club emerged. It has been a challenge and a pleasure to write about the unpredictable, talented, and feisty membership of the Badminton and Racquet Club of Toronto.

Mary Byers

Bibliography

Canadian Encyclopedia, Volume I. Edmonton. Hurtig. 1985

Canadian Lawn Tennis and Badminton. Volume VII, No. 5 February 1935

Filey, Mike *The TTC Story – The First Seventy-Five Years.* Toronto. Dundurn Press, 1996

Kinsella, Joan C. *Historical Walking Tour of Deer Park.* Toronto Public Library, 1996

Mutimer, Brian. *History of Squash Racquets in Canada.* Edmonton. William A. Dowbiggin, 1988

Transit in Toronto. Toronto Transportation Commission, 1976. Revised 1982

Toronto Street Directories 1922-1927

Who's Who in Canada. Toronto: Hodder and Stoughton 1927-1948

Magazines and Research papers

Squash Ontario Volume 1, No. 4 March/April 1978, Volume 1 No. 5 Summer Edition 1978

Squash Life Volume 7, No. 6 Nov./Dec. 1983

Research papers on the history of Toronto. D. Rodwell Austin, author with Ted Barris of *Carved in Granite, 125 years of Granite Club History*, Macmillan, 1999

Research resources of the City of Toronto/TTC Archives

Index

Names have been indexed as in the text, which is for the most part in the familiar form. Captions under the photographs have not been indexed.

Adamson, Sara 116, 131
Andrewes, Cyril K.F. 26, 28, 39
Armour, Mr. and Mrs. Eric 21
Armour, John, 121
Armstrong, Jeffrey 106
Armstrong, Marion 24, 25
Ashworth, Mr. and Mrs. J.J. 21

Baldwin, Mrs. W. 21
Bacque, Mr. 127
Bacque, Mrs. 127
Baird, Chuck 98, 100
Baird, Norma 98, 100
Baldwin, Eric 126
Mrs. W. Baldwin 21
Balfour, St. Clair 76, 104
Ballon, Eddie 130, 199, 200
Ballon, Heather 199
Barnard, Peter 78, 79, 88, 110-112, 114
Barrett, Bill 85
Bassett, David 69, 71, 79, 80, 125
Bassett, Doug 113
Bassett, John 70, 78, 79, 88, 96
Bassett, John Sr 71, 96
Baxter, Major and Mrs. 21
Beardmore, Mrs. Torrance 21
Beatty, Geoff 65
Bedard, Bob 84, 121

Behan, Conor 127
Behan, Susan (McElhinney) 71, 72, 94, 108, 121
Bell, Barbara (Cooper) 88
Bell, Bessie Hildegarde Brooke (Blackstock) 15, 49
Bell, Mrs. 127
Bewley, Bill 75
Bigelow, H. (Ned) 67, 68
Birch, Dick 51
Birks, Mr. and Mrs. 21
Bishop, Arthur 31, 90
Black, Geoff 79
Blackstock, Bessie Hildegarde Brooke (Bell) 15, 49
Blackstock, Harriet Victoria (Gooderham) 13
Blackstock, Lieutenant-Colonel George Gooderham 13-15, 17-19, 21, 26-31, 48, 49, 101
Blackstock, Thomas Gibbs 13
Blaikie, Ann 24
Boake, Patty 200
Bocquet, Derek 64, 70, 75-79, 81, 82, 86, 88, 91, 92, 96, 100, 106, 109, 111, 121
Boone, Major Charles 21
Boone, Mrs. Charles A. (Dorothy) 17, 21, 24, 26, 29, 41, 46, 60, 74, 103
Bosley, William 17
Boulevard Club, The 30, 60
Boulton, Bill 30
Boulton, Peter 30
Bower, Doug 122, 130, 200
Boynton, Doug 57
Boynton, John 71, 110
Boynton, Tom 57, 69, 70
Brauns, W. Stewart Jr 67

Brightling, David 122, 137, 199
Brock, Mildred 50
Brouse, Mrs. Eaton 21
Brown, Doug 125
Brown, Mr. and Mrs. R.C. 21
Brown, Arthur 36, 51
Buchanan, Mrs. James 21
Buchanan, Roy Beresford 13, 16-19, 21, 30, 39, 51, 90
Buckman, Kate 86
Bull, Perkins 43

Cadieux, Stephane 126
Canadian Army Medical Corps Badminton Club 17
Canadian Platform Tennis Association, The 96
Carlton Club, The 15, 25, 34, 52, 60
Carpenter, Mr. and Mrs. 21
Carr-Harris, Mr. and Mrs. 21
Carter, J. Scott 31
Cassels, Lou Anne 103
Cawthra, Miss Isobel 21
Chan, Leo 122
Chapman, Smith 79
Cheesbrough, Gord 110
Chipman, John H. "Jack" 31, 40, 65
Christie, Mr. and Mrs. Huntley 21
Clark, Christie 21, 36, 65
Clark, Mrs. Christie 21
Clarke, Mrs. T.J. 21
Coke, Cherith (Howard) 27, 61
Coke, Mrs. E.F. (Esme) 16, 21, 24, 25-27, 29, 34, 39, 46, 50, 60, 103
Cook, Gordon 25, 46, 52
Cooper, Ann 102, 105
Cooper, Barbara (Bell) 88
Corcoran, Maggie 73, 102, 103, 121, 199
Corcoran, Terry 70, 89, 125

Crean, Jack 46, 51, 60
Crossley, Susan (Wansbrough) 95, 127
Crowther, Miss 21
Crowther, Mr. and Mrs. 21
Currelly, Mrs. 127
Currie, George 98, 118
Cutts, Charlie 51, 75
Cutts, Stan 51

D'Aguanno, John 120
Dack, Geraldine 16
Davey, Michael 86
Davidson, Pam 94, 96
Dawson, Harry 129
De Pencier, John 83, 111, 132
Deck, Fran 83
Deeks, Ed 30
Doherty, Nancy 83, 98, 99, 104, 106
Donalda Club, The 119
Douglas, Howard 44
Douglas, Mrs. Howard 43
Drew, Premier George 14, 49
Duggan, Mike 36, 43, 59
Dunning, Paul 107, 108 114, 126, 199
Dyment, Mr. 127

Eastmure, Esther (Jackson) 54, 104
Eaton, Alan 45, 60
Eaton, Mrs. E.Y. 21
Eaton, Mrs. J. W. 87
Edgar, Miss Grace 21
Edgar, Mrs. James 21
Ellis, Mr. 127
Elmsley, Miss 21
Evans, Gay 105
Evans, Gill 115, 131

Evans, Mr. and Mrs. George 21

Fairty, Mrs. 127
Falconer, Elsie 112, 113, 124
Fauquier, Harry 79, 80, 88, 93, 100
Fergusson, Blair 73
Fergusson, Mrs. "Elf" 73, 127
Finch, Ken 82
Finlayson, R.W. 52, 87
First, Daphne, (Walker) 54, 55
Fisher, Gordon 98
Fisher, Ruby 40, 53, 57, 87
Fleming, Chink 58, 98, 100, 122, 125, 127
Flemming Paul 24, 42, 51, 127
Foy, John 64, 69-71, 75, 81, 88, 94, 106, 199
Fraser, John 133
Fraser, Ramsey 31, 32, 50, 59, 65, 133
Fraser. Dr. 59
Frontier Club, The 15

Garden, Jane 19, 61
Garden, Murray 17, 19, 21, 47, 188
Gardiner, Mrs. 41
Geale, Bev 52, 60
George, Dr. Ruggles 21
George, Mrs. Ruggles 17, 21, 26
Gibson, Pam 105
Gilbert, Humphrey 100
Gillespie, Jay 100
Gilmour, John 30
Glassco, Willa 103
Godfrey, Mary 103
Gooderham, Harriet Victoria (Blackstock) 13
Gooderham, Mrs. J. Leys (Olive) 17, 21, 24, 41, 61, 74
Gooderham, Mrs. W. 21
Gooderham, Peter 59, 69

Gooderham, The Misses 21
Gordon, Mary (Nunns) 78-81, 98, 99
Gordon, Peter 92, 97
Gouinlock, Mrs. 127
Gould, Ruth (Wansbrough) 95, 127
Granite Club, The 30, 33, 52, 55, 60, 70, 72, 107, 108, 122
Grant, Bob 52, 80, 82, 83, 87
Grant, Doug 99, 100, 110
Grant, Marney (Lace) 43, 52
Grant, Ruth (Nunns) 79, 98, 99, 131
Gray, O.E. (Tim) 24, 25, 32, 40, 41, 46, 51, 65, 75
Greey, Ann (Richmond) 54, 55, 58, 61, 96, 200
Greey, Paul 65
Greey, Philip A. 67, 69
Griffin, Scott 28
Guest, Valerie 102
Gundy, Fred 46, 59, 69, 100
Gunn, Lew 71

Haldenby, Doug 112
Halder, Greg 92, 93
Halder, Wally 57, 80, 81, 87
Ham, Art 80
Hamilton Squash Racquets Club, The 66
Hamilton, Doug 57, 60, 65, 68, 69
Hamilton Thistle Club, The 51, 71, 75, 77
Hammond, Diane 82, 127
Hanley, Peter 69
Harding, Victor 52, 69, 71, 93, 96, 100, 126
Harris, Naomi "Pick" 74
Harrison, Bruce 76, 83, 87, 88, 127
Harrison, "Pooh" (Sidney) 85
Hatch, Bill 69, 71
Hatcher, Peter 71, 98, 99, 121-123, 131
Heighington, Mary 103, 104
Heintzman, Annabelle 103, 104, 106, 110, 199

Heintzman, Barbara 71
Heintzman, Bill 110, 124
Heisey, Larry 100
Henderson, George 85
Henderson, H.A. 39
Henderson, Nancy 71, 72, 121
Henderson, Paul 100
Hennessey, Joan 54, 55
Higginbotham, David 67, 69, 111, 115, 122, 131, 132
Hildick-Smith, Peter 69
Howard, Cherith (Coke) 27, 61
Howard, Ernie 51, 57, 59, 61, 64, 67-70, 74, 81, 88, 89, 199
Howard, Mr. and Mrs. S. 21
Howe, Mrs. Lyman 86, 127
Humphrey, Mrs. 127
Hunter, Elizabeth 86
Hunter, Margaret "Pug" 58, 85
Hutchinson, Julien 71
Hydro Electric Power Commission of Ontario 17

Ireton, John 69
Ireton, Mrs. 127
Irwin, Steve 110, 111
Islington Golf and Country Club, The 114

Jablonsky, Milan 115, 118, 119
Jack, Richard RA 49
Jackson, Commander T.J. 51-53, 57, 59, 64, 82, 87, 90, 127
Jackson, Esther (Eastmure) 54, 104
Jackson, Jakey 34
Jarvis "Deacon" 59
Jarvis, Mrs. Edgar 21
Jarvis, Strachan 127
Jarvis, Wendy 123, 200
Jennings, Doug 71
Jones, Elijah 96, 98

Jones, Mel 69, 88

Kennedy, J. de N. 17, 21, 26
Kent, Mary 103
Khan, Hashim 70
King, C.M. "Mac" 57, 90
Kingstone, Mrs. George 21
Kingsway Club, The 96, 99
Kirby, Major 51
Kitchener-Waterloo Racquet Club, The 107
Knowles, Mary 96, 118
Korthals, Judy 72, 105

Lace, Barbara 43
Lace, Frank 30, 32
Lace, Marney (Grant) 43, 52
Laidlaw, Mr. and Mrs. R.A. 21, 127
Lancaster, H.D. 65
Langford, Lieutenant-Colonel and Mrs. 21
Langmuir, Ken 82
Lapham, Henry 66
Larkin, Gerald 21, 87, 106
Larkin, Harley W. 19
Larkin, Mr. and Mrs. Harold 21
Lawson, H.H. 56,
Lee, Joe 51
Lee, Mr. and Mrs.Cecil 51
Leggat, Don 71, 75
Leishman, Mrs. 127
Lima, Maria 114
Lind, Emmy 105
Logie, Robin 71, 133
Longmore, Norman 57, 87, 98, 109, 127
Lownsbrough, Tim 45, 52, 60

Mabee, Barbara 88

MacCracken, Cal 67, 68
Macdonald, David 133
Macdonnell, Rayne 50, 53
MacKenzie, Sir William 28
MacPhail, Stephen 127
Magann, Mr. and Mrs. George 21
Maier, Dick 118, 121
Manning, Mrs. 42
Manning, Trevor 34, 42, 51
Mansell, J.Roy 121
Mansfield, George 108
Mara, George 57
Marshall, Edith 54
Martin Kathy (Vernon) 110
Martin, Mrs. Leslie 21
Martin, Walter 38, 80
Massey, The Right Hon Vincent and Mrs Massey 101
Mason, Mrs. Douglas 21
May, Jack 57, 88
Mayfair Club, The 108
Maynard, Jock 57, 61, 69, 96
McCann, Pat 109, 114, 122
McCarthy, Tom 87, 122
McCausland, John K. "Jack" 40, 65, 69, 74
McClelland, Skee 102, 117, 118
McElhinney, Patricia 72
McElhinney, Susan (Behan) 71, 72, 94, 108, 121
McGill University 66
McKay, Heather 125
McLaggan, Doug 64, 69
McLeod, Anne 105
McMurrich, Jim 69
McMurrich, Ted 85
McPherson, Pam (Westcott) 46, 60, 96
McWhinney, Mrs. 21
Michener, Roland, The Right Hon. 101

Mills, Willo 86
Minton, Bill 69, 71
Mitchell, Bev 34
Mitchell, Mrs. G.G. 21
Moffatt, Don 134, 199
Montreal Amateur Athletic Association, The 70
Montreal Cricket Club, The 76
Montreal Badminton and Squash Club, The 64, 70
Montreal Racket Club, The 66
Morgan, Sandy 94, 96, 106, 108
Morton, Joanne 52, 82, 87, 88, 127
Moysey, Warren 118, 199
Munro, Bill 102, 104, 105, 107, 110-112, 134, 199
"Murphy" 76, 82, 83, 92, 114, 116, 121, 136, 137
Musgrave, Doug 82, 91

Nanton, the Misses 21
New York City Badminton Club, The 30
Niagara Falls Country Club 53
Nicholls, Mr. and Mrs. Walter 21
Nixon, Joe 85, 190
Northey, Margot (Nunns) 88
Nunns, Bea (Symons) 80, 81, 86,
Nunns, Brenda (Shoemaker) 79, 80
Nunns, Gilbert 39, 76, 80-82, 121
Nunns, Margot (Northey) 88,
Nunns, Mary (Gordon) 78-81, 98, 99
Nunns, Ruth (Grant) 79

Oakville Club, The 30
O'Gorman, Eleanor 107, 108, 114, 116, 118,126, 199
O'Rorke, Pam 99
Oakley, Mr. 127
Ondaatje, Chris 100
Ormsby, Tony 121
"Otto" 64, 81

Parker, Betty 71
Parker, Bill 53
Parmenter, Reginald 21
Peterson, Harold 65, 69
Philp, Jane (Wansbrough) 95, 127
Philpott, Douglas 74
Pinkerton, Bill 45, 60
Pinkham, John 96, 108
Pipon, Miss 21
Porter, Budd 53, 54, 96
Proctor, Barbara 37, 41, 44, 45, 88, 199
Proctor, John 30, 57, 61, 90
Proctor, Mr. and Mrs. A.H.C. "Dolly" 21, 87, 100, 106
Purcell, Bill 53
Purcell, Jack 13, 51

Radcliffe, C.C. 65
Reaves, Mrs. Campbell 21
Reburn, Dudley 52, 58
Redfern, Don 102, 105, 106
Richardson, John 134
Richmond, Ann (Greey) 54, 55, 58, 61, 96, 200
Ridley College 66
Risdon, Mrs. 127
Rober, Howie 71, 133
Robertson, Margaret 34
Rodziunas, Dana 120
Ross, Mr. and Mrs. Douglas 21
Royal Canadian Yacht Club, The 44
Royal Military College 13, 14
Russell, David 25, 46, 47, 60

Sabina, Nancy 86
Salmond, Hope 40, 50, 57, 101, 116
Savage, Mr. and Mrs. 21

Scandrett, Bill 45, 52, 60
Scarboro Golf and Country Club, The 109
Seagram, Bill 46, 59
Seagram, Norman 37, 102
Seymour, Harry 85
Seymour, Lil 85
Shoemaker Brenda (Northey) 79, 80
Short, Jeff 69
Suckling, Miss 21
Sinclair, Ken 108
Sisam, Sue 115, 123
Skillman, John 67
Smart, Dr. Sydney 118
Smith, Burke 68
Smith, Lyman 93
Smythe, Don 53, 54
Snell, Colonel A.E. 30
Sniffen, Ronald 30
Sommerville, Sandy 68
Southam, Bud 30
Springer, Bob 57
Squibb, Morris 51, 52, 87
St. George's Golf Club 122
Stephenson, Mrs. 127
Stevenson, David 115
Stewart, Ian 64, 68-70, 74, 81, 92, 109
Stewart, Joan 73, 75, 103
Stewart, Peter 70, 71, 75, 87, 88, 94, 97
Stock, Val 110
Stowe, Betsy 103
Strathgowan Club, The 60
Stuart, Jim 85, 96
Suydam, Mrs. J.C 34, 127
Symons, Bea (Nunns) 80, 81, 86,

Taylor, Barry 82, 95

Taylor, John M. "Jack" 26, 38, 39, 52, 57
Taylor, Mary 71
Telfer, Elizabeth 102, 103
Thomas, Sir George, Baronet 28
Thompson, Ann 65, 94
Thompson, Fred 105
Thomson, William Raymond 19
Tilden, Bill 81
Toronto Cricket, Curling and Skating Club, The 75
Toronto Garrison Badminton Club, The 13, 16
Toronto Hunt Club, The 46
Toronto Lawn Tennis Club, The 76, 101, 114
Toronto Racquet Club, The 13, 19, 31, 65, 66
Toronto Transportation Commission 9, 17
Torrance, Fred 46, 59, 60
Townley Peter 102, 110
Traviss, Jim 68, 73
Traviss, Judy 71, 72, 80, 82, 87, 94
Trinity College School 66

University Club, The 13, 31, 65
University of Toronto, The 9, 14, 56, 66, 81, 107, 122
Upper Canada College 13, 66, 121

Vernon, Kathy (Martin) 110
Victoria Club, The 43

Walker, Daphne, (First) 54, 55
Walker, Martin 98, 99
Walsh, Miss Margaret 21
Walton, Dorothy 52, 60
Wansbrough, Ruth (Gould) 95, 127
Wansbrough, Jane (Philp) 95, 127
Wansbrough, Susan (Crossley) 95, 127
Waterloo Tennis Club, The 107
Watson, Alan 110, 149

Watson, Graeme 13, 16 29, 36, 39, 65, 72, 90
Watson, Peter 39, 65, 72
Watt, Sandy 59, 198
Wedd, William Basil 19
Weir, John 105
Welch, Winifred 71
Wells, Tony 71, 106, 108, 125, 128-131
Welsman, Carol 135
Westcott, Bev 30, 46, 50, 53, 54, 60, 68, 82, 96, 199
Westcott, Pam (McPherson) 46, 60, 96
Whelpton, Ernie 71, 76, 93, 100
Whelpton, Jennifer 118
Whitaker, Dennis 71
White, Jim 21, 59
White, Karen 71
White, Mrs. James 21
Wickett, Alice (Allie-Mo) 103
Wigmore, Lieutenant Commander 87
Wilder, Billy 56, 103
Wills, Gordon 59
Wilson, Bill 92
Wilson, Charles Lesslie 19, 21
Wilson, Mrs. C. Lesslie 21, 37
Wilson, R.F. 58, 148
Wingfield, Major 76
Winter Club, The 13
Wise, Dick 121
Woodcock, Canon 40
Wright, Susan 110
Wrong, Mrs. Hume 21

York Club, The 30, 52, 60
York Badminton Club, The 40

Zeidler, Jane 105